Healing
Scriptures
and
Prayers

JEFF DOLES

Healing Scriptures and Prayers
©2003 by Jeff Doles

ISBN-10: 0-9744748-1-9
ISBN-13: 978-0-9744748-1-6

Published by
Walking Barefoot Ministries
P.O. Box 1062, Seffner, FL 33583

Cover design and book interior by www.ChristianBookDesign.com

For more resources on enjoying new life in Christ, living in faith and the power of the Holy Spirit, or to find out more about Jeff Doles, visit our websites:

www.WalkingBarefoot.com
www.TheFaithLog.com
www.JeffDoles.com

Contents

I am the LORD *who heals you.*

Exodus 15:26

Introduction

Someone has said that prayer is not about overcoming God's reluctance but about laying hold of His willingness. This can also be said of healing ministry—it is not about overcoming God's reluctance, but laying hold of His willingness to heal. God's willingness to heal is seen in His Word, where He has repeatedly revealed His desire to heal His people. This book is designed to help you lay hold of God's willingness to heal you by laying hold of His Word and praying it back to Him.

The Scriptures

Most of the Scriptures in this book directly relate to healing. Some are included because they demonstrate God's continuing desire to bless His people in every way. Others are included because they relate to the operation of faith—an important factor in receiving healing.

Read these healing Scriptures out loud, so that your eyes see them, your mouth speaks them, your ears hear them, your body feels the rhythm of the words, and your mind perceives them. More importantly, keep reading them and let the words penetrate into your heart and into your spirit.

The Bible says that "Faith comes by hearing, and hearing by the Word of God" (Romans 10:17). This happens by an action of the Holy Spirit, so ask the Holy Spirit to make these Scriptures come alive inside you. Then begin to speak them out in faith. Jesus said that the mouth speaks out of the abundance of the heart.

The Word of God reveals the will of God, and so enables us to pray effectively. "Now this is the confidence that we have in Him, that if we ask anything according to His will, He hears us. And if we know that He hears us, whatever we ask, we know that we have the petitions that we have asked of Him" (1 John 5:14-15). Healing is the will of God for His people, as these Scriptures show, so pray confidently, knowing that He hears you, and that you will receive your healing.

The Prayers

As you welcome the Word of God and meditate on it, and faith begins to stir in your heart, start praying the Word back to Him. This honor's God because His Word reveals His heart, and when you pray it back to Him, your heart begins to line up with His. Remember that you are not just seeking the healing, you are seeking the Healer.

The prayers in this book are designed to help you exercise your faith and pray the healing Scriptures back to God. Faith comes by hearing, but it is exercised by what you say, and by what you pray. Jesus said that faith is like a mustard seed—it is not the size that is important, its what you do with it. A seed must be planted, and prayer is one way to do that.

These prayers do not include, "if it be Thy will." This is because the will of God concerning healing has been made known, as the healing Scriptures in this book attest. "If it be Thy will" is appropriate for prayers of dedication or consecration, but not for prayers of healing, where the will of God has already been revealed.

Don't feel limited by these prayers. They are merely examples to give you a place to begin. They are a framework to lend you support, not a structure to confine you. So feel free to alter, expand or discard them as you will. The important thing is to respond with faith to the healing Word of God. If you would like to use these prayers to pray for healing for someone else, simply insert his or her name wherever appropriate.

When you begin praying, don't be in a hurry. Take your time and pray slowly. As you do, you may find that you feel an inward desire to expand upon some particular point. That is the Holy Spirit prompting you, and if you listen carefully, He will give you words to pray back to the Father. Go with this as far as the Spirit leads you. When you come to the end, sit quietly and contemplate what the Spirit has given you. If you wish, you can pick up the prayer where you left off, and continue until the Spirit gives you more. When you come to the end of your prayer time, simply give thanks and praise to God and welcome His healing power at work in your life.

- Take these Scriptures like medicine. Read them regularly and meditate on them as much as you can. The more you let them fill your heart, the more your faith will grow, and the more effective (and joyful) your prayers will be.
- Prayer is not magical, nor is it mechanical. It is a vital and ongoing relationship with the Lord. Faith is not positive thinking. Positive thinking is about what *we can do*. Faith is about believing God and what *He has said.*
- Pray these prayers by faith, not by sight. What you experience with your senses must eventually line up with the truth of God's Word.
- These prayers are not intended to replace your current treatment. If you are on medication, do not quit taking it until you have seen your doctor and he has confirmed your healing.
- Pray in expectation. Watch for your healing, not for the symptoms of sickness. Begin to do things you could not do before.
- If there is any unconfessed sin in your life, it may be an obstacle to your healing, so bring it to the Lord. "If we confess our sins, He is faithful and just to forgive us our sins and to cleanse us from all unrighteousness" (1 John 1:9). Repentance is a wonderful thing because it is an opportunity to begin again.
- Forgive others. Lack of forgiveness can hinder your prayers, and so hinder your healing. Jesus said, "Whenever you stand praying, if you have anything against anyone, forgive him, that your Father in heaven may also forgive you your trespasses" (Mark 11:25).
- In the healing ministry of Jesus, sometimes there were demonic forces at work behind various sicknesses and conditions, and Jesus had to expel these in order to bring about healing. If you have reason to suspect that such forces may be involved in your illness, you may need to seek out help from someone who is experienced in deliverance ministry.

One Final Word

This book assumes that the reader has received the Lord Jesus Christ and is born again by the Spirit of God. This is important because the ministry of Jesus on the Cross is the basis for all healing. The Bible says, "For I am not ashamed of the Gospel of Christ, for it is the power of God to salvation, for everyone who believes" (Romans 1:16). The Greek word for "salvation" is *sozo* and means to save, heal, deliver, make whole and preserve.

The Bible says, "If you confess with your mouth the Lord Jesus and believe in your heart that God has raised Him from the dead, you will be saved. For with the heart one believes unto righteousness, and with the mouth confession is made unto salvation" (Romans 10:9-10). With the heart we believe, with the mouth we confess. That is how faith works.

If you have never received the Lord Jesus Christ and experienced new life in Him, you can do it right now. Let this simple prayer be a guide:

Dear Lord,

I confess that I am a sinner and that I have come short of your glory. But I believe that You love me and that Jesus died on the Cross for my sins. I confess with my mouth that Jesus is Lord, and believe in my heart that You have raised Him from the dead. I now receive Your wonderful gift of salvation through Jesus Christ my Lord, and I ask you to fill me with Your Holy Spirit.

In Jesus' name, Amen.

If you prayed that prayer and meant it in your heart, you have just entered into a new and wonderful relationship with God. All the blessings and promises of God, and the saving benefits of the Lord Jesus Christ belong now to you.

Receive your healing now—in Jesus' name.

Old Testament Healing Scriptures

The LORD Who Heals

I am the LORD who heals you. (Exodus 15:26)

So you shall serve the LORD your God, and He will bless your bread and your water. And I will take sickness away from the midst of you. No one shall suffer miscarriage or be barren in your land; I will fulfill the number of your days. (Exodus 23:25-26)

And the LORD will take away from you all sickness, and will afflict you with none of the terrible diseases of Egypt which you have known. (Deuteronomy 7:15)

Thus says the LORD ... "I have heard your prayer, I have seen your tears; surely I will heal you." (2 Kings 20:5)

Dear Lord,
I give You thanks and praise. You are my Lord, and I take joy in serving You. You bless my bread and my water, and You take sickness far away from me. I thank You that You hear my prayer and see my tears. I thank You that healing is mine, and the number of my days will be fulfilled, for You are the Lord who heals me.
In Jesus' name, Amen.

You have granted me life and favor,
    and Your care has preserved my spirit.

(Job 12:10)

Healing Scriptures from the Psalms

Blessed is the man who walks not
    in the counsel of the ungodly,
    nor stands in the path of sinners,
    nor sits in the seat of the scornful;
But his delight is in the law of the LORD,
    and in His law he meditates day and night.
He shall be like a tree planted by the rivers of water,
    that brings forth its fruit in its season,
    whose leaf also shall not wither,
    and whatever he does shall prosper.

(Psalm 1:1-3)

God's desire is for you to have "whole-life" prosperity—prosperity in your inner being, in your body, and in your circumstances. The Apostle John expressed the will of God when he wrote, "Beloved, I pray that you may prosper in all things and be in health, just as your soul prospers" (3 John 2).

Dear Lord,

I delight in Your Word and in Your ways. As I meditate upon them day and night, I become like a well-watered tree, planted and established beside the rivers of God. I shall bring forth fruit in season—the overflow of abundant life! My leaf will not wither but shall be fresh and green. Thank You for prosperity in every area of my life—spirit, soul and body.

In Jesus' name, Amen.

The LORD is my Shepherd, I shall not want.
He makes me to lie down in green pastures;
    He leads me beside the still waters.
He restores my soul.
He leads me in the paths of righteousness
    for His name's sake.

Yea, though I walk through the valley of the shadow of death,
I will fear no evil, for You are with me.
Your rod and Your staff, they comfort me.
You prepare a table before me
in the presence of my enemies.
You anoint my head with oil. My cup runs over.
Surely goodness and mercy shall follow me
all the days of my life;
And I will dwell in the house of the LORD forever.

(Psalm 23)

I will extol You, O LORD, for You have lifted me up,
and have not let my foes rejoice over me.
O LORD my God, I cried out to You, and You healed me.
O LORD, You brought my soul up from the grave;
You have kept me alive,
that I should not go down to the pit.

(Psalm 30:1-3)

Whoever of you loves life,
and desires to see many good days
Keep your tongue from evil,
and your lips from speaking lies.
Turn from evil and do good;
seek peace and pursue it.

(Psalm 34:12-14 *NIV*)

Yes, Lord,

I love life and desire to see many good days. Help me keep my tongue from speaking evil and my lips from mouthing lies. Help me turn from evil and do good. Help me seek Your peace and pursue it in every circumstance. Thank You for giving me long life filled with Your goodness.

In Jesus' name, Amen.

Many are the afflictions of the righteous,
but the LORD delivers him out of them all.

(Psalm 34:19)

How blessed is he who considers the helpless;
>   the LORD will deliver him in a day of trouble.
The LORD will protect him and keep him alive,
>   and he shall be called blessed upon the earth ...
The LORD will sustain him upon his sickbed;
>   in his illness, You restore him to health.

(Psalm 41:1-3 NASB)

Dear Lord,

Bless me as I consider the helpless, the poor and the weak. Remember me as I remember them. Deliver me in the day of trouble. Protect me and keep me alive, that I may be blessed upon the earth. Sustain me upon this sickbed and restore me to health. Your healing power is far greater than my afflictions, and I know You will deliver me from them all.

In Jesus' name, Amen.

God is our refuge and strength,
>   a very present help in trouble.

(Psalm 46:1 NIV)

I will cry out to God Most High,
>   to God who performs all things for me.
He shall send from heaven and save me.

(Psalm 57:2-3)

Dear God,

I cry out to You—my refuge and my strength. My help in time of trouble. I look to You to accomplish everything that needs to be done for me. I thank You that You send forth Your healing word from heaven to save me and make me whole.

In Jesus' name, Amen.

Blessed be God, Who has not turned away my prayer,
>   nor His mercy from me!

(Psalm 66:20)

Blessed be the Lord,
>   Who daily loads us with benefits,
>   the God of our salvation!

(Psalm 68:19; the *NIV* says, "Who daily bears our burden.")

Blessed are You, O Lord my God,
For You have not turned away my prayer, nor Your faithful love and mercy
from me. Daily You bear my burdens. Daily You load me with benefits. Thank
You for Your healing touch.

In Jesus' name, Amen.

For the LORD God is a sun and shield;
the LORD will give grace and glory;
no good thing will He withhold
from those who walk uprightly.
O LORD of hosts, blessed is the man who trusts in You!

(Psalm 84:11-12)

"Sun" speaks of life and restoration: "But to those who fear My name,
the Sun of Righteousness shall arise with healing in His wings" (Malachi
4:2). "Shield" speaks of protection. The words for "grace and glory" are
rendered in the NIV as "favor and honor." In the Bible, glory and honor
are often tangible manifestations.

Dear Lord,
You are my sun and shield, my restorer and my protector. You show me grace
and favor, and give me glory and honor. No good thing do You withhold from those
who walk in Your ways. I am blessed, and healing is mine, because I trust in You.

In Jesus' name, Amen.

He who dwells in the secret place of the Most High
shall abide under the shadow of the Almighty.
I will say of the LORD, "He is my refuge and my fortress;
my God, in Him I will trust."
Surely He shall deliver you from the snare of the fowler
and from the perilous pestilence.

(Psalm 91:1-3)

Dear Lord,
I will dwell in Your presence and rest in Your shade, for You are my refuge

and my fortress. You are my God, I run to You. I trust You, Lord, for You deliver me from the snare, and from terrible, destructive disease.

In Jesus' name, Amen.

Because you have made the LORD, who is my refuge,
 even the Most High, your dwelling place,
No evil shall befall you,
 nor shall any plague come near your dwelling;
For He shall give His angels charge over you,
 to keep you in all your ways.

(Psalm 91:9-11)

Dear Lord,

 I thank You that no evil shall befall me, that no plague has a right to come near my house, for You are my refuge. Thank You for Your angels to guard and protect me.

In Jesus' name, Amen.

Because he has set his love upon Me,
 therefore I will deliver him;
I will set him on high, because he has known My name.
He shall call upon Me, and I will answer him;
 I will be with him in trouble;
 I will deliver him and honor him.
With long life I will satisfy him,
 and show him My salvation.

(Psalm 91:14-16)

O Jesus,

 I love You and cling to You with all my heart. With joy I call out Your name—Jesus! Thank You for being with me in trouble, for delivering me and honoring me. Thank You for satisfying me with long life and for showing me Your salvation.

Amen.

The righteous shall flourish like a palm tree,
 he shall grow like a cedar in Lebanon.

Those who are planted in the house of the LORD
    shall flourish in the courts of our God.
They shall still bear fruit in old age;
    they shall be fresh and flourishing,
    to declare that the LORD is upright;
He is my rock, and there is no unrighteousness in Him.

(Psalm 92:13-15)

The Bible says that God made Jesus, "who knew no sin to be sin for us, that we might be made the righteousness of God in Him" (2 Corinthians 5.21). In God's eyes, those who trust in Jesus are thus made righteous, and are eligible for every blessing that belongs to the righteous.

Dear Lord,

Thank You for the Lord Jesus Christ, who took my sin upon Himself and gave me Your righteousness. Thank You for establishing me in Your house, where I can flourish in Your courts. Even in old age I shall be fresh and green—still bearing fruit. For You are my rock, and You are righteous in all Your ways.

In Jesus' name, Amen.

Bless the LORD, O my soul; and all that is within me,
    bless His holy name!
Bless the LORD, O my soul, and forget not all His benefits:
Who forgives all your iniquities,
Who heals all your diseases,
Who redeems your life from destruction,
Who crowns you with lovingkindness and tender mercies,
Who satisfies your mouth with good things,
So that your youth is renewed like the eagle's.

(Psalm 103:1-5)

With everything that is within me, I bless You, O Lord.

I remember all the benefits You have for me. You forgive all my sins and heal all my diseases. You redeem my life from destruction and crown me with demonstrations of Your love and kindness and tender mercies. You satisfy my desires with good things and renew my youth like the eagle's. Thank You for my healing.

In Jesus' name, Amen.

He also brought them out with silver and gold,
    and there was none feeble among His tribes.

(Psalm 105:37)

Then they cried out to the LORD in their trouble,
    and He saved them out of their distresses.
He sent His word and healed them,
    and delivered them from their destructions.

(Psalm 107:19-20)

Dear Lord,

I cry out to You to save me in my distress and deliver me from destruction. I believe that when You deliver Your people, there is no lack of resources and no feebleness of health. Thank You for sending Your word to heal me.

In Jesus' name, Amen.

Gracious is the LORD, and righteous;
    yes, our God is merciful.
The LORD preserves the simple;
    I was brought low, and He saved me.
Return to your rest, O my soul,
    for the LORD has dealt bountifully with you.
For You have delivered my soul from death,
    my eyes from tears, and my feet from falling.
I will walk before the LORD
    in the land of the living.

(Psalm 116:5-9)

Dear Lord,

You are gracious and righteous in all Your ways, and Your mercy is very great. My soul finds rest in You, for You have dealt bountifully with me. You have delivered my soul from death, my eyes from tears, my feet from falling. With joy and thanksgiving I walk before You in the land of the living. Thank You for my healing.

In Jesus' name, Amen.

I shall not die, but live, and declare the works of the LORD.

(Psalm 118:17)

Remember the word to Your servant,
　　upon which You have caused me to hope.
This is my comfort in my affliction,
　　for Your word has given me life.

(Psalm 119:49-50)

He heals the brokenhearted and binds up their wounds.

(Psalm 147:3)

Dear Lord,

Thank You for Your Word. Your life-giving promises comfort me in my affliction. I watch for them in joyful anticipation. Thank You for healing my broken heart and binding up my wounds. I shall not die, but live, and tell everyone what You have done for me.

In Jesus' name, Amen.

Healing Scriptures from Proverbs

My son, do not forget my teaching,
　　but keep my commands in your heart,
For they will prolong your life many years
　　and bring you prosperity.

(Proverbs 3:1-2 *NIV*)

Do not be wise in your own eyes;
　　fear the LORD and depart from evil.
It will be health to your flesh,
　　and strength to you bones.

(Proverbs 3:7-8)

My son, give attention to my words;
　　incline your ear to my sayings.
Do not let them depart from your eyes;
　　keep them in the midst of your heart;
For they are life to those who find them,
　　and health to all their flesh.
Keep your heart with all diligence,

17

for out of it spring the issues of life.

(Proverbs 4:20-23)

Dear Lord,

Your word prolongs my life, and brings me peace and prosperity. I will give attention to Your sayings and keep them in my heart, for they are life to me, and health to my body. I will obey Your commands and walk in Your ways, for they are strength to my bones. I will carefully watch over my heart to honor You in all things, for the health of my body is related to the wholeness of my soul. Thank You for my healing.

In Jesus' name, Amen.

The fear of the LORD is the beginning of wisdom,
    and the knowledge of the Holy One is understanding.
For by me your days will be multiplied,
    and years of life will be added to you.

(Proverbs 9:10-11)

Dear Lord,

You are awesome to me. I honor You with my whole heart. I love what You love and I hate what You hate. I want You more than anything else, and to lose You would be the greatest tragedy of my life. Lord, give me wisdom and understanding by Your Holy Spirit, that I may know You more and more, and I will rejoice in You all my days.

In Jesus' name, Amen.

Reckless words pierce like a sword,
    but the tongue of the wise brings healing.

(Proverbs 12:8 *NIV*)

A heart at peace gives life to the body,
    but envy rots the bones.

(Proverbs 14:30 *NIV*)

A wholesome tongue is a tree of life,
    but perverseness in it breaks the spirit.

(Proverbs 15:4)

Pleasant words are like a honeycomb,

sweet to the soul and healing to the bones.

(Proverbs 16:24 *NIV*)

The Bible says, "Finally, brethren, whatever things are true, whatever things are noble, whatever things are just, whatever things are pure, whatever things are lovely, whatever things are of good report, if there is any virtue and if there is anything praiseworthy—meditate on these things" (Philippians 4:8).

A merry heart does good, like medicine,
  but a broken spirit dries the bones.

(Proverbs 17:22)

The tongue has the power of life and death,
  and those who love it will eat its fruit.

(Proverbs 18:21 *NIV*)

Dear Lord,
  I ask You for a wise tongue and a heart at peace, for they are life and healing to me. I will meditate on pleasant words—things that are true and noble and just and pure and lovely and of good report, things that are virtuous and praiseworthy. With my mouth I will speak words of life and wholeness, and give thanks to You for my healing.
  In Jesus' name, Amen.

Healing Scriptures from the Prophets

And it shall come to pass in that day, that his burden shall be taken away from off thy shoulder, and his yoke from off thy neck, and the yoke shall be destroyed because of the anointing. (Isaiah 10:27 *KJV*)

Jesus is the Anointed One of God (Hebrew *Messiah*, Greek *Christ*). His anointing removes every burden laid on us by the oppressor and obliterates every yoke of bondage. Neither sickness, nor poverty, nor oppression can stand against the Anointed One and His anointing.

Dear Lord,
  I thank You that You have anointed Jesus to completely remove every burden of sickness and utterly destroy every bondage of disease in my life. Your anointing brings

healing and wholeness to me. Thank You for Your grace and mercy in my life.
In Jesus' name, Amen.

Those who wait on the LORD shall renew their strength; they shall mount up with wings like eagles, they shall run and not be weary, they shall walk and not faint. (Isaiah 40:31)

Fear not, for I am with you; be not dismayed, for I am your God. I will strengthen you, yes, I will help you, I will uphold you with My righteous right hand. (Isaiah 41:10)

Dear Lord,
I look to You in patient expectation. Renew my strength like the wings of eagles. Help me and uphold me by the power of Your might. Then I shall go forth in strength and wholeness. I shall run and not be weary; I shall walk and not faint. Thank You for my healing.
In Jesus' name, Amen.

Surely He has borne our griefs and carried our sorrows; yet we esteemed Him stricken, smitten by God, and afflicted. But He was wounded for our transgressions, He was bruised for our iniquities; the chastisement for our peace was upon Him, and by His stripes we are healed. (Isaiah 53:4-5)

These "griefs" and "sorrows" are actually *infirmities, sicknesses, diseases* and *pains*. That is why Matthew applied this passage to the healing ministry of Jesus, observing that Jesus "healed *all* the sick" who were brought to Him:

When evening had come, they brought to Him many who were demon-possessed. And He cast out the spirits with a word, and healed all who were sick, that it might be fulfilled which was spoken by Isaiah the prophet, saying: "He Himself took our infirmities and bore our sicknesses" (Matthew 8:16-17).

Dear Lord Jesus,
Thank You for bearing all my infirmities, all my sicknesses, all my diseases, and all my pains. Thank You for suffering the judgment for all my sins. You were

chastised so I could receive Your peace and wholeness, and by Your stripes I am healed.

Amen.

"No weapon formed against you shall prosper, and every tongue which rises against you in judgment you shall condemn. This is the heritage of the servants of the LORD, and their righteousness is from Me," says the LORD. (Isaiah 54:17)

> Sickness is a weapon fashioned and used by the enemy to come against the child of God. For the devil is a thief, who comes to steal, kill and destroy God's people (John 10:10).
>
> The child of God is one who walks, not in his own righteousness, but in the righteousness of the LORD. "For He [God] made Him [Jesus] who knew no sin to be sin for us, that we might become the righteousness of God in Him" (2 Corinthians 5:21).
>
> The Hebrew word for "righteousness" is *tsedeq* and also refers to prosperity. The one who walks in the righteousness of the LORD prospers in the LORD. That is why no weapon of the enemy can prosper against him. It cannot stand up against the prosperity of God.

Dear Lord,

Thank You for the righteousness of the Lord Jesus Christ now at work in me. I receive the heritage of the servants of the Lord. I walk in the righteousness that comes from the Lord, I overcome with the prosperity of the Lord. No weapon formed against me shall prosper—not even sickness or disease, for I belong to the Lord. Thank You for my healing.

In Jesus' name, Amen.

For as the heavens are higher than the earth, so are My ways higher than your ways, and My thoughts than your thoughts. For as the rain comes down, and the snow from heaven, and do not return there, but water the earth, and make it bring forth and bud, that it may give seed to the sower and bread to the eater, so shall My word be that goes forth from My mouth; it shall not return to Me void, but it shall accomplish what I please, and it shall prosper in the thing for which I sent it. (Isaiah 55:9-11)

Dear Lord,

I say "Yes" to Your ways and Your thoughts, for they are true and powerful and greater than any sickness or disease. Thank You for Your life-giving word that accomplishes Your purposes upon the earth and in my life. Thank You for sending Your word to heal me.

In Jesus' name, Amen.

"I have seen his ways, and will heal him; I will also lead him, and restore comforts to him and to his mourners. I create the fruit of the lips: Peace, peace to him who is far off and to him who is near," says the LORD, "And I will heal him." (Isaiah 57:18-19)

> This passage is directed to the backslider who returns to the Lord in faith and obedience. The Bible says, "If we confess our sins, He is faithful and just to forgive us our sins and to cleanse us from all unrighteousness" (1 John 1:9). In his penitence, David said, "Create in me a clean heart, O God, and renew a steadfast spirit within me" (Psalm 51:10).

Dear Lord,

Is there any sin in my life that I have not yet confessed? Please show me now and help me to repent. [Pause for a moment to listen.]

Forgive me, Lord, and cleanse me from all unrighteousness. Create in me a clean heart, O God, and renew a steadfast spirit within me. Thank You for giving me peace. Thank You for giving me a fresh start. Thank You for healing me.

In Jesus' name, Amen.

Is this not the fast that I have chosen: to loose the bonds of wickedness, to undo the heavy burdens, to let the oppressed go free, and that you break every yoke?

Is it not to share your bread with the hungry, and that you bring to your house the poor who are cast out; when you see the naked, that you cover him, and not hide yourself from your own flesh?

Then your light shall break forth like the morning, your healing shall spring forth speedily, and your righteousness shall go before you; the glory of the LORD shall be your rear guard. Then you shall call, and the LORD will answer; you shall cry, and He will say, 'Here I am.'

If you take away the yoke from your midst, the pointing of the finger, and speaking wickedness, if you extend your soul to the hungry and satisfy the afflicted soul, then your light shall dawn in the darkness, and your darkness shall be as the noonday.

The LORD will guide you continually, and satisfy your soul in drought, and strengthen your bones; you shall be like a watered garden, and like a spring of water, whose waters do not fail. (Isaiah 58:6-11)

Dear Lord,

Help me to share my bread with the hungry, to show hospitality to the poor and compassion to the needy. O God who is Love, I repent of my selfish ways and give myself whole-heartedly to Your compassionate ways. Thank You for hearing my cry and answering my call. Thank You for satisfying my soul and strengthening my bones. Thank You for healing me.

In Jesus' name, Amen.

Heal me, O LORD, and I shall be healed; save me, and I shall be saved, for You are my praise. (Jeremiah 17:14)

For thus says the LORD ... "I will visit you and perform My good word toward you. For I know the thoughts that I think toward you," says the LORD, "thoughts of peace and not of evil, to give you a future and a hope. Then you will call upon Me and go and pray to Me, and I will listen to you. And you will seek Me and find Me, when you search for Me with all your heart. I will be found by you," says the LORD. (Jeremiah 29:10-14)

"For I will restore health to you and heal you of your wounds," says the LORD. (Jeremiah 30:17)

Behold, I will bring ... health and healing; I will heal them and reveal to them the abundance of peace and truth. (Jeremiah 33:6)

Dear Lord,

I thank You that Your thoughts toward me are peace and wholeness—to give me a hope and a future. With joy, I call on Your name. Help me to seek after You with my whole heart. Thank You for restoring my health and healing my wounds, and for revealing the abundance of Your peace and truth in my life.

In Jesus' name, Amen.

The LORD is good to those who wait for Him, to the soul who seeks Him. It is good that one should hope and wait quietly for the salvation of the LORD. (Lamentations 3:25-26)

I will seek what was lost and bring back what was driven away, bind up the broken and strengthen what was sick. (Ezekiel 34:16)

But to you who fear My name the Sun of Righteousness shall arise with healing in His wings; and you shall go out and grow fat like stall-fed calves. (Malachi 4:2)

Yes Lord,

You are good to those who seek You, to those who revere Your name. You seek what is lost and restore what is scattered. You bind up the broken and give strength to the sick. I wait quietly and with joyful expectation for Your salvation to appear. Thank You for Jesus, the Sun of Righteousness, who is risen with healing—my healing—in His wings. I shall leap exuberantly like a calf from the stall and praise Your name forever.

In Jesus' name, Amen.

Healing Names of God

There are many names in the Old Testament by which God reveals Himself in ways that directly, or indirectly, concern healing. Many of these are combinations based on His personal name, Yahweh (or Jehovah), the name by which He relates to His people and reveals His purposes. Others are combinations based on El, the Hebrew word for "God," the name by which He displays His power. These names demonstrate both the greatness and the goodness of God. Not only does God desire wholeness for His people, He is completely able to bring it about.

The Bible says, "For whoever calls on the name of the Lord shall be saved" (Romans 10:13). The Greek word for "saved" is *sozo* and means to be saved, healed, delivered, restored, made whole. We receive these saving benefits by coming into agreement with His name. The Bible says, "Therefore by Him let us continually offer the sacrifice of praise to God, that is, the fruit of our lips giving thanks to His name" (Hebrews 13:15). The Greek for "giving thanks" is *homologeo* and means to confess, or agree with. When we call on the name of the Lord, giving thanks to His name, we are exercising faith, agreeing with who He is and how He has revealed Himself. In this way, the names of God become pathways of healing.

The LORD Will Provide
Yahweh Yireh

And Abraham called the name of the place, *The LORD Will Provide.*

(Genesis 22:14)

The root word of *yireh* is *ra'ah*, which literally means "to see." God beholds and perceives. *Ra'ah* signifies, not merely the nearness of God, but shows that He is present to provide whatever is needed. God *sees* the need and moves to meet it. In Genesis 22, God saw the need for a sacrifice to be offered in place of Isaac, so He provided a ram, ultimately pointing toward the sacrifice of the Lord Jesus Christ in our place.

But Isaac spoke to Abraham his father and said, "My father!" And he said, "Here I am, my son." Then he said, "Look, the fire and the wood, but where *is* the lamb for a burnt offering?" And Abraham said, "My son, God will provide [*ra'ah*] for Himself the lamb for a burnt offering." (Genesis 22:7-8).

God has seen your need for healing and has already made provision for it. John the Baptist saw Jesus and declared, "Behold! The Lamb of God who takes away the sin of the world!" (John 1:29). Jesus Himself is the provision of God who opens the way for us to receive every blessing of God, including healing. Call on His name as Your healing provider.

O Lord My Provider,

Thank You for seeing my need and making provision for my healing. Thank You for the Lord Jesus, the Lamb of God who takes away my sin and opens the way for me to receive every blessing. Thank You for forgiving my sins and for meeting every need. Thank You for my healing.

In Jesus' name, Amen.

The LORD Who Heals You
Yahweh Rapha

If you diligently heed the voice of the Lord your God and do what is right in His sight, give ear to His commandments and keep all His statues, I will put none of the diseases on you which I have brought on the Egyptians. For I am *The Lord Who Heals You.* (Exodus 15:26)

By this name, *Yahweh Rapha*, God reveals Himself as the One who brings healing to all those who heed His voice and walk in His ways. *Rapha* means to mend, cure, heal, repair and make whole.

Psalm 103 says, "Bless the LORD O my soul ... who forgives all your iniquities, who heals all your diseases" (vv. 2-3). In Psalm 107:20, God sent His word and healed those who cried out to Him. Psalm 147 declares that the LORD "heals the brokenhearted and binds up their wounds" (v. 3). Isaiah spoke of Messiah and "the day that the LORD binds up the bruise of His people and heals the stroke of their wound" (Isaiah 30:26).

Luke 4 records that, when Jesus began His public ministry, He read from the scroll of Isaiah (61:1-2):

The Spirit of the LORD is upon Me,
　　Because He has anointed Me
To preach the gospel to the poor;
　　He has sent Me to heal the brokenhearted,
To proclaim liberty to the captives
　　And recovery of sight to the blind,
To set at liberty those who are oppressed;
　　To proclaim the acceptable year of the LORD.

(Luke 4:18-19)

Jesus closed the scroll, sat down and declared, "Today, this Scripture is fulfilled in your hearing." In this way, Jesus revealed Himself as our healer.

O Lord My Healer,

　　Thank You for sending Your word to make me whole. Thank You for forgiving all my sins and healing all my diseases. Thank You for anointing Jesus to mend my broken heart and bind up my wounds. You give sight to the blind and freedom to the captive. Today, this Scripture is fulfilled and I declare that I am healed.

In Jesus' name, Amen.

The LORD is My Banner
Yahweh Nissi

And Moses built an altar and called its name, *The LORD is My Banner.*
(Exodus 17:15)

Moses built an altar of thanksgiving after the Lord gave victory to the children of Israel over the Amalekites. He called it *Yahweh Nissi*, for the Lord is a banner of victory and truth, a rallying place for His people. David said, "You have given a banner to those who fear You, that it may be displayed because of the truth" (Psalm 60:4).

When the Lord is our banner, victory is assured. Paul said, "If God be for us, who can be against us?" (Romans 8:31). The healing that God brings is far greater than any sickness or disease the devil brings. "In all these things, we are more than conquerors through Him who loved us" (Romans 8:37). "Thanks be to God, who gives us the victory through our Lord Jesus Christ" (1 Corinthians 15:57).

In the Song of Solomon, the banner is a symbol of intimacy between the LORD and His bride. "He brought me to the banqueting house, and his banner over me was love" (2:4). "God so loved the world that He gave His only begotten Son" (John 3:16). Jesus is not only our victory banner, He is the banner of God's love over us, and the emblem of our healing.

O Lord My Banner
You are my victory and the One who loves me. Thank You for sending Jesus into the world as the banner of Your love, to heal me and give me victory over every disease and affliction. I receive Your healing love now.
In Jesus' name, Amen.

The LORD Who Sanctifies You
Yahweh Qadesh

I am *The LORD Who Sanctifies You.* (Exodus 31:13)

To be sanctified means to be cleansed and made holy, set apart for God's special purposes and promises. It is signified by anointing oil. David said to the Lord, "You anoint my head with oil" (Psalm 23:5). Another psalm

28

writer declared, "I have been anointed with fresh oil" (Psalm 92:11).

Isaiah prophesied, "It shall come to pass in that day that [the oppressor's] burden will be taken away from your shoulder, and his yoke from your neck, and the yoke will be destroyed because of the anointing oil" (Isaiah 10:27). The anointing removes the oppressive burden of sickness and destroys the yoke of disease.

James said, "Is anyone among you sick? Let him call for the elders of the church, and let them pray over him, anointing him with fresh oil" (James 5:14). The anointing oil is a sign of God's sanctifying and healing presence.

Sanctification is for the entire person, and includes healing for the body. Paul said, "Now may the God of peace Himself sanctify you completely; and may your whole spirit, soul, and body be preserved blameless at the coming of our Lord Jesus Christ. He who calls you is faithful, who also will do it" (1 Thessalonians 5:23-24).

O Lord Who Sanctifies Me,

Thank You for cleansing me and setting me apart for Your wonderful purposes and promises. You have anointed me with fresh oil, an anointing which completely removes the burden of sickness and destroys the yoke of disease in my life. Thank You for making me whole—spirit, soul and body.

In Jesus' name, Amen.

The LORD is Peace
Yahweh Shalom

So Gideon built an altar there to the LORD, and called it *The LORD is Peace.*

(Judges 6:24)

The *shalom*, or peace of God, is wholeness and well-being. It signifies health, prosperity, safety, wellness, restoration and joy. God desires to bless His people with peace, as we see in the Aaronic blessing: "The LORD lift up His countenance upon you, and give you peace" (Numbers 6:26).

David said, "I will both lie down in peace, and sleep; for You alone, O LORD, make me dwell in safety" (Psalm 4:8). "The LORD will give strength to His people; the LORD will bless His people with peace" (Psalm 29:11).

In Isaiah, the Lord promises "You shall go out with joy, and be led out with peace" (Isaiah 55:12). This is possible because of what the Lord Jesus did, for as Isaiah prophesied about the Messiah, "The chastisement of our peace was upon Him" (Isaiah 53:5). A great exchange has taken place—Jesus was chastised in our place so that we might experience His peace and wholeness in our lives. He took our sin and gave us His righteousness. He took our sicknesses and pains and gave us His healing and health.

O Lord My Peace,

Thank You for looking upon me with Your favor and giving me Your peace. You make me dwell in safety and You bless me with wholeness. Thank You, Lord Jesus, for bearing my sin and my sickness on the Cross, that I may have Your life and health at work in my body. I receive it now.

In Jesus' name, Amen.

The LORD of Hosts
Yahweh Sabaot

The LORD of Hosts is with us; the God of Jacob is our refuge.

(Psalm 46:7)

The Lord of Hosts is the name by which God wages warfare on behalf of His people. He reveals Himself as our faithful defender, and the one who establishes justice for us. There is also an indication of intimacy associated with this name, for He is identified as our Redeemer. "Thus says the LORD, the King of Israel, and his Redeemer, the LORD of hosts" (Isaiah 44:6). "As for our Redeemer, the LORD of hosts is His name" (Isaiah 47:4). More specifically, He is our Kinsman Redeemer (Hebrew *ga'al*), that is, one who acts on behalf of his next of kin, to ransom, redeem, or deliver. A kinsman redeemer would buy back his relative's property or marry his widow, for the sake of the family and to protect their inheritance.

The LORD of Hosts is also identified as our husband. "For your Maker is your husband, the LORD of hosts is His name" (Isaiah 54:5). We see the healing significance of this name in the prayer of Hannah, who cried out to the Lord in her barrenness, "O LORD of hosts, if You will indeed look on the affliction of Your maidservant and remember me, and not forget Your maidservant, but will give Your maidservant a male child, then I will give him to the LORD all the days of his life." (1 Samuel 1:11).

Jesus is the LORD of hosts, our kinsman redeemer. He is the faithful husband who defends and delivers us in every situation, bringing healing and restoration for barrenness and every sickness.

O Lord of Hosts,

My Defender, my Kinsman, my Redeemer. You have fought the battle for me, and in Your justice I am made whole. You have taken my barrenness and given me fruitfulness and abundance. Under Your protection I am healed and fully restored.

In Jesus' name, Amen.

The LORD is My Shepherd
Yahweh Rohe

The LORD is my Shepherd; I shall not want. (Psalm 23:1)

The shepherd takes care of the sheep, providing for every need. He satisfies their hunger in fresh, green pastures. He quenches their thirst and refreshes them beside calm, cooling waters. He restores them to wholeness. He guides and protects them, and leads them safely through the valley of the shadow of death.

Isaiah said of Messiah, "He will feed His flock like a shepherd; He will gather the lambs with His arms, and carry them in His bosom" (Isaiah 40:11).

Jesus said, "I am the good shepherd. The good shepherd gives His life for the sheep" (John 10:11). The devil is a false shepherd, a thief who comes only to steal, kill and destroy the sheep. But "I have come," Jesus said, "that they may have life, and that they may have it more abundantly" (John 10:10).

Jesus is our Shepherd, who brings us the abundant life of God. There is healing and wholeness in Him, and no lack at all.

O Lord My Shepherd,

How faithful are Your lovingkindnesses and tender mercies. You satisfy my desires with good things and give me peaceful rest in green pastures. You refresh and restore me beside calming waters. You lead me and protect me all along the way. You prepare a table of bounty for me, even as my enemies look on. You anoint me with fresh oil and I am filled with Your abundance. Goodness and mercy are my constant companions. I am made whole and lack for nothing, for You are my Shepherd.

In Jesus' name, Amen.

The LORD Our Righteousness
Yahweh Tsidkenu

"Behold, the days are coming," says the LORD, "that I will raise to David a Branch of righteousness; a King shall reign and prosper, and execute judgment and righteousness in the earth. In His days Judah will be saved, and Israel will dwell safely. Now this is His name by which He will be called: *The LORD Our Righteousness.*" (Jeremiah 23:5-6)

The Hebrew word for righteousness, *tsedeq*, speaks of that which is altogether right and just. It also refers to prosperity. Righteousness is God's way of doing and being right. It is His "rightness." When we walk in this rightness, we experience His blessing and prosperity. Psalm 112, for example, describes at length the blessing and prosperity of those who are righteous.

Jesus is the Branch of David, the King who reigns and prospers. He is our righteousness. "For He [God] made Him [Jesus] who knew no sin to be sin for us, that we might become the righteousness of God in Him" (2 Corinthians 5:21). Therefore, we are eligible for every blessing and benefit that belongs to the righteous (see Deuteronomy 28). Sickness and disease belong to the curse, but healing and wholeness belong to the blessing—and the blessing belongs to the righteous.

O Lord My Righteousness,
Thank You for the Lord Jesus Christ, who is my righteousness. Thank You for every blessing and benefit that belongs to the righteous. I receive them now. Healing is mine, prosperity is mine, and all the good things of God are mine, for in Jesus I am made right with God.

In Jesus' name, Amen.

The LORD is There
Yahweh Shammah

And the name of the city from that day on shall be: *The LORD is There.*

(Ezekiel 48.35)

Looking toward a time of healing and restoration, the Book of Ezekiel closes with this name, *Yahweh Shammah*, "The LORD is There." It is a name which signifies the glory of the Lord, His divine presence manifesting in power and purity. It is a healing presence, for there is no more place in it for sickness or disease than there is for sin. They are overtaken by healing and wholeness. David could well say, "You will show me the path of life; in Your presence is fullness of joy" (Psalm 16:11).

Jesus brings this joyful, life-giving presence of God close to us. "Behold, the virgin shall be with child, and bear a Son, and they shall call His name Immanuel," which is translated, "God is with us" (Matthew 1:23). Jesus said, "He who has seen Me has seen the Father" (John 14:9). Paul added, "For in Him [Jesus] dwells all the fullness of the Godhead bodily" (Colossians 2:9). This fullness dwells in us, for God has revealed to us a great mystery, "which is Christ in you, the hope of glory" (Colossians 1:27). All the fullness of God dwells in Christ, and all the fullness of Christ dwells in us.

O Lord Who is There,

Thank You for Your presence, Your power and Your purity. You show me the path of life, and in Your presence is fullness of joy. Thank You for the Lord Jesus Christ, who dwells in me with all the fullness of God. Thank You for His healing presence. Sickness now goes and healing now comes, for You are here with me.

In Jesus' name, Amen.

Almighty God
El Shaddai

The LORD appeared to Abram and said to him, "I am *Almighty God*; walk before Me and be blameless. And I will make My covenant between Me and you, and will multiply you exceedingly. (Genesis 17:1-2).

God revealed Himself to Abram (Abraham) as *El Shaddai,* Almighty God, and made a covenant with him. Abraham confirmed this covenant to Isaac, and Isaac confirmed it to Jacob: "May God Almighty bless you, and make you fruitful, and multiply you ... and give you the blessing of Abraham" (Genesis 28:3). Likewise, Jacob spoke the blessing of *El Shaddai* over his son Joseph:

> By the God of your father who will help you,
>   And by the Almighty who will bless you
> With blessings of heaven above,
>   Blessings of the deep that lies beneath,
> Blessings of the breasts and of the womb.
>
> (Genesis 49:25)

In the book of Job, righteous Elihu understood *El Shaddai* as the one who gives, sustains and restores life. "The Spirit of God has made me, and the breath of the Almighty gives me life" (Job 33:4). This is the Hebrew *chayah*—life preserved, life repaired, life made whole.

El Shaddai is a refuge in time of trouble, as the psalmist knows. "He who dwells in the secret place of the Most High shall abide under the shadow of the Almighty" (Psalm 91:1).

All who believe in the Lord Jesus Christ are in covenant with Almighty God. We are part of the "multiplication of Abraham" and heir with him to all the blessings of God. *El Shaddai* is faithful to His covenant. He is our continual refuge in every need, and He is mighty to sustain and restore us to wholeness.

Almighty God,

My covenant God, You are faithful. You give me life, You sustain me, You restore me. You are my refuge. I abide in the shade of Your presence and I am made whole. You multiply me and give me increase. You bless me. By Your covenant faithfulness, You prove again and again that You are El Shaddai, Almighty God.

In Jesus' name, Amen.

Everlasting God
El Olam

Then Abraham planted a tamarisk tree in Beersheba, and there called on the name of the LORD, the *Everlasting God.* (Genesis 21:33)

The covenant God made with Abraham is everlasting. "I will establish My covenant between Me and you and your descendants after you in their generations, for an everlasting [*olam*] covenant, to be God to you and your descendants after you" (Genesis 17:7).

Those who believe in the Lord Jesus Christ are called descendents of Abraham. "And if you are Christ's, then you are Abraham's seed, and heirs according to the promise" (Galatians 3:29). In Christ, we are heirs to an everlasting covenant with an everlasting God.

The psalm writer declared, "The Lord is good; His mercy is everlasting [*olam*]" (Psalm 100:5). God's mercy (Hebrew, *hesed*) is His covenant love and faithfulness. He has committed Himself to our well-being, and He will not break His promise. Not ever!

Everlasting God,

You are good and Your mercy endures forever. You keep Your word to all generations. In Your covenant love, I am made whole. All the blessings of Abraham are mine, for You are El Olam, the Everlasting God.

In Jesus' name, Amen.

God Most High
El Elyon

I will cry out to *God Most High,*
To God who performs all things for me.
He shall hear from heaven and save me:
He reproaches the one who would swallow me up.
God shall send forth His mercy and His truth.

(Psalm 57:2-3).

God Most High is the name which shows that He is Lord over all. The Most High is the possessor of heaven and earth (Genesis 14:19,22). He establishes the inheritance and boundaries of the nations (Deuteronomy 32:8). He is the source of knowledge, revelation and counsel (Numbers 24:16; 2 Samuel 22:14; Psalm 107:11).

The Most High is King over all the earth (Psalm 47:2), but He is also a refuge and fortress to deliver us from sickness and disease:

He who dwells in the secret place of the Most High
    shall abide under the shadow of the Almighty.
I will say of the LORD, "He is my refuge and my fortress;
    My God, in Him I will trust."
Surely He shall deliver you from the snare of the fowler
    and from the perilous pestilence ...
Because you have made the LORD, who is my refuge,
    even the Most High, your dwelling place,
No evil shall befall you,
    nor shall any plague come near your dwelling.

                 (Psalm 91:1-3, 9-10)

David said, "I will cry out to God Most High, to God who performs all things for me." God Most High performs all things for us. To perform means to bring to completion. God will bring us to completion in every area of our life. There is no situation God cannot handle, no need He will not meet. He delivers us from every evil. Therefore, we can confidently call on Him to deliver us from every plague and heal us from every disease.

Jesus is God Most High, for He is seated at the right hand of the Father, "far above all principality and power and might and dominion, and every name that is named, not only in this age but also in that which is to come" (Ephesians 1:21). "Therefore God also has highly exalted Him and given Him the name which is above every name" (Philippians 2:9). The name of Jesus is far above the name of cancer, heart disease, diabetes, and every other sickness that can be named. He is Lord over all.

God Most High,

    You are my refuge, my fortress, my dwelling place. I cry out to You to do all that needs to be done for me. I trust in You to heal me and make me whole.

    My Jesus, You are Lord over all, seated at the right hand of the Father. Your name and authority are far greater than any sickness or disease. Therefore, with confidence, I look to You for my healing, and I receive it now.

                 In Jesus' name, Amen.

The Living God
El Hay

My heart and my flesh cry out for the *Living God.*

(Psalm 84:2)

God, like His Word, is "living and powerful" (Hebrews 4:12). He is *El Hay*, the living God. To speak this name is to speak of His awesomeness. "For who is there of all flesh who has heard the voice of the living God speaking from the midst of the fire, as we have, and lived?" (Deuteronomy 5:26).

The Bible says, "It is a fearful thing to fall into the hands of the living God" (Hebrews 10:31). But for those who know Him and call on His name, the living God is the God of life! "We trust in the living God, who is the savior of all men, especially of those who believe" (1 Timothy 4:10). Paul called Him "the living God, who gives us richly all things to enjoy" (1 Timothy 6:17). "All things" includes life, healing and wholeness.

Those who trust in Him are children of the living God. "And it shall come to pass in the place where it was said to them, 'You are not my people,' there it shall be said to them, 'You are the sons of the living God" (Hosea 1:10). God will not withhold healing from His children.

The Bible says that we are the dwelling place for the God of life. "For you are the temple of the living God" (2 Corinthians 6:16). This means life for us, "For He is not the God of the dead but of the living" (Luke 20:38). We have the very principle of life—the God of life and the life of God—at work in us. Therefore, we do not need to tolerate sickness in our bodies any more than we need to tolerate sin in our lives, for the holy God who lives in us is also living and powerful, able to heal as well as sanctify.

Jesus is the living God. Speaking by the Holy Spirit, Peter declared, "You are the Christ, the Son of the living God" (Matthew 16:16). In contrast to the devil, who comes to steal, kill and destroy, Jesus comes to bring us the very life of God, and to give it to us in abundance (John 10:10).

My Living God,
In You there is no death. In You there is no sickness. In You there is no disease. In You there is life and healing and wholeness. I rejoice to be Your child and Your dwelling place.

O Jesus, You came that I might have life, and that I might have it more abundantly. Your life—the very life of God—is now at work in my body, and I am made healthy and whole. All things are now mine, richly to enjoy, for You are the God of my life. I give You thanks and praise.

In Jesus' name, Amen.

God Who Forgives
El Nasa

You answered them, O LORD our God;
   You were to them *God-Who-Forgives.*

(Psalm 99:8)

The name God-Who-Forgives expresses, not only forgiveness of sins, but healing of sicknesses and diseases, as well. There has always been a close connection between the two. David said, "Bless the LORD, O my soul, and forget not all His benefits: Who forgives all your iniquities; Who heals all your diseases" (Psalm 103:2-3).

The messianic portrait in the book of Isaiah shows that Jesus bore both our sins and our sicknesses. "Surely He has borne our griefs [literally "sicknesses"] and carried our sorrows [literally "pains"] ... He was wounded for our transgressions, He was bruised for our iniquities; the chastisement of our peace was upon Him, and by His stripes we are healed" (Isaiah 53:4-5).

When Jesus healed the paralytic man, in Luke 5, He said, "Man, your sins are forgiven you." Then, so the scribes and Pharisees would realize that He indeed has authority to forgive, Jesus said to the man, "Arise, take up your bed, and go to your house." The man received both forgiveness of sins and physical healing.

James said, "The prayer of faith will save the sick, and the Lord will raise him up. And if he has committed sins, he will be forgiven. Confess your trespasses to one another, and pray for one another, that you may be healed" (James 5:15-16). The God who forgives our sins is the same God who heals our afflictions.

God Who Forgives,
   With all that is in me, I give You thanks and praise, and I remember all

Your benefits. Lord Jesus, You bore all my sins and sicknesses in Your body on the Cross, and I thank You that You have forgiven all my iniquities and healed all my diseases.

In Jesus' name, Amen.

Other Healing Names of God

I will love You, O Lord, my strength. The Lord is my rock and my fortress and my deliverer; my God, my strength, in whom I will trust; my shield and the horn of my salvation, my stronghold. (Psalm 18:1-2)

There are many other names in the Old Testament by which God reveals Himself in a healing way:

- Faithful God (Deuteronomy 7:9)
- Strength of My Life (Psalm 27:1)
- God of My Strength (Psalm 43:2)
- God of My Salvation (Psalm 88:1)
- God My Helper (Psalm 54:4)
- Help of My Countenance (Psalm 42:11)
- Balm in Gilead (Jeremiah 8:22)
- Sun of Righteousness (Malachi 4:2).

I love You, O Lord, my strength,
  You are my rock, my fortress, my deliverer;
  My God, my strength, in whom I will trust;
  My shield and the horn of my salvation, my stronghold.

Almighty and Everlasting God,
  Forever and ever, You remain the same, perfect in power, love and purity. Nothing is too great for Your power. Nothing is too small for Your lovingkindness and tender mercies.

O Lord, my God,
  You are my Provider, who saw my need and moved to meet it.
  You are my Healer, who heals all my diseases.
  You are my Victory Banner, the sign of my healing.

You are my Sanctifier, the Anointed One who lifts my burden and destroys my yoke.

You are my Peace, who makes me whole—nothing missing, nothing broken.

You are my Shepherd, who gives me rest in green pastures and restores my soul beside calm waters.

You are my Righteousness, who reconciles me to the Father and qualifies me for all the blessings of heaven and earth.

You are the Lord Who is There for me in every circumstance of life. I rejoice in Your presence, for You heal me and restore me in every way.

With all my heart, I bless You, O Lord,

I will remember all Your benefits and give You thanks and praise. For You are great, and You are good, and I love Your name forever.

In Jesus' name, Amen.

Choosing Life

Our God is a God of covenant. By His name, *Yahweh*, He entered into covenant with the children of Israel. As they prepared to enter ther Promised land, God renewed His covenant with them. The book of Deuteronomy is the document of that renewal, and it is laid out in the form of a covenant.

In Deuteronomy 28, God proclaimed a series of blessings and curses. If His people obeyed His voice and kept His commandments, they would experience the blessing of God in every single area of their lives. This is found in the first fourteen verses:

> Now it shall come to pass, if you diligently obey the voice of the Lord your God, to observe carefully all His commandments which I command you today, that the Lord your God will set you high above all nations of the earth.
>
> And all these blessings shall come upon you and overtake you, because you obey the voice of the Lord your God:
>
> Blessed shall you be in the city, and blessed shall you be in the country.
>
> Blessed shall be the fruit of your body, the produce of your ground and the increase of your herds, the increase of your cattle and the offspring of your flocks.
>
> Blessed shall be your basket and your kneading bowl.
>
> Blessed shall you be when you come in, and blessed shall you be when you go out.

The LORD will cause your enemies who rise against you to be defeated before your face; they shall come out against you one way and flee before you seven ways.

The LORD will command the blessing on you in your storehouses and in all to which you set your hand, and He will bless you in the land which the LORD your God is giving you.

The LORD will establish you as a holy people to Himself, just as He has sworn to you, if you keep the commandments of the LORD your God and walk in His ways.

Then all peoples of the earth shall see that you are called by the name of the LORD, and they shall be afraid of you.

And the LORD will grant you plenty of goods, in the fruit of your body, in the increase of your livestock, and in the produce of your ground, in the land of which the LORD swore to your fathers to give you.

The LORD will open to you His good treasure, the heavens, to give the rain to your land in its season, and to bless all the work of your hand. You shall lend to many nations, but you shall not borrow.

And the LORD will make you the head and not the tail; you shall be above only, and not be beneath, if you heed the commandments of the LORD your God, which I command you today, and are careful to observe them.

So you shall not turn aside from any of the words which I command you this day, to the right or the left, to go after other gods to serve them. (Deuteronomy 28:1-14)

If the people of Israel chose not to hear the voice of the Lord or obey His commands, they would not be positioned to experience His blessing. Outside the blessing, there is nothing left but the curse. This is detailed in Deuteronomy 28:15-68. Here are the portions that pertain to the area of sickness and health:

But it shall come to pass, if you do not obey the voice of the LORD your God, to observe carefully all His commandments and His statutes which I command you today, that all these curses will come upon you and overtake you. (v. 15)

The LORD will make the plague cling to you until He has consumed you from the land which you are going to possess. The LORD will strike you with consumption, with fever, with inflammation, with severe burning fever. (vv. 21-22)

The LORD will strike you with the boils of Egypt, with tumors, with the scab, and with the itch, from which you cannot be healed. The LORD will strike you with madness and blindness and confusion of heart. (vv. 27-28)

The LORD will strike you in the knees and on the legs with severe boils which cannot be healed, and from the sole of your foot to the top of your head. (v. 35)

If you do not carefully observe all the words of this law that are written in this book, that you may fear this glorious and awesome name, THE LORD YOUR GOD, then the LORD will bring upon you and your descendants extraordinary plagues—great and prolonged plagues—and serious and prolonged sicknesses. Moreover He will bring back on you all the diseases of Egypt, of which you were afraid, and they shall cling to you. Also, every sickness and every plague, which is not written in this Book of the Law, will the LORD bring upon you until you are destroyed. (vv. 58-61)

Notice that sickness and disease belong to the curse, not to the blessing. Notice also that this requires a choice on the part of God's people. This choice is presented even more explicitly a few chapters later:

I call heaven and earth as witnesses today against you, that I have set before you life and death, blessing and cursing; therefore choose life, that both you and your descendants may live; that you may love the LORD your God, that you may obey His voice, and that you may cling to Him, for He is your life and the length of your days; and that you may dwell in the land which the LORD swore to your fathers, to Abraham, Isaac, and Jacob, to give them." (Deuteronomy 30:19-20)

Outside the covenant blessing of God, there is nothing to look forward to except plague, consumption, fever, inflammation, severe burning fever, boils, tumors, scab, incurable itch, madness, blindness, confusion of heart, severe boils on knees and legs—from the soles of the feet to the top of the head, extraordinary plagues, great and prolonged plagues, serious and prolonged sickness, all the diseases of Egypt, and every plague and sickness not mentioned here by name.

But for those who choose life and blessing, the picture is completely different. No sickness, no disease, no madness of the mind, no confusion of the heart. Living in the blessing of God brings health, wholeness, prosperity and peace.

God gives the choice: "I have set before you life and death, blessing and cursing." He even reveals the correct answer: "Therefore, choose life."

A New and Better Covenant

This was the covenant God made with the children of Israel in the Old Testament. It is not the covenant made with Abraham, although it is based upon it. Rather, it is the covenant made under the leadership of Moses. The problem, though, was that the nation and people of Israel repeatedly disobeyed God, forgot His ways and broke covenant with Him. Thus, they repeatedly brought curse upon themselves. That is why God began speaking of a *new* covenant:

> "Behold, the days are coming," says the LORD, "when I will make a new covenant with the house of Israel and with the house of Judah—not according to the covenant that I made with their fathers in the day that I took them by the hand to lead them out of the land of Egypt, My covenant which they broke, though I was a husband to them," says the LORD. "But this is the covenant that I will make with the house of Israel after those days, says the LORD: I will put My law in their minds, and write it on their hearts; and I will be their God, and they shall be My people. No more shall every man teach his neighbor, and every man his brother, saying, 'Know the LORD,' for they all shall know Me, from the least of them to the greatest of them," says the LORD. "For I will forgive their iniquity, and their sin I will remember no more." (Jeremiah 31:31-34)

This new covenant is fulfilled in the Lord Jesus Christ. First, He has redeemed us from the curse of the old Mosaic covenant, including all the sickness and disease brought on by that curse. He did this by becoming a curse for us.

Christ has redeemed us from the curse of the law, having become a curse for us (for it is written, "Cursed is everyone who hangs on a tree"), that the blessing of Abraham might come upon the Gentiles in Christ Jesus. (Galatians 3:13-14).

Not only did Jesus become a curse, that the power of the curse over us might be broken, He also became sin that the power of sin over us might be broken. "For He [God] made Him [Jesus] who knew no sin to be sin for us, that we might become the righteousness of God in Him" (2 Corinthians 5:21).

Jesus instituted the new covenant, a covenant based on the shedding of His blood at the Cross. We see this in the institution of the Lord's Supper.

And as they were eating, Jesus took bread, blessed and broke it, and gave it to them and said, "Take, eat; this is My body." Then He took the cup, and when He had given thanks He gave it to them, and they all drank from it. And He said to them, "This is My blood of the new covenant, which is shed for many." (Mark 14:22-24)

As great as the Old Testament covenant under Moses was, and as wonderful as all of its blessings were, the author of Hebrews declares that the *new* covenant in Jesus' blood is even better. "But now He has obtained a more excellent ministry, inasmuch as He is also Mediator of a better covenant, which was established on better promises" (Hebrews 8:6).

When we receive the Lord Jesus Christ, we enter into a new covenant and a new righteousness. This is not a covenant we keep for ourselves, for that is something we could never accomplish. The good news of the Gospel is that Jesus has already accomplished it for us. He became sin for us so that we could become the very righteousness of God in Him. We receive this righteousness through faith in Him. Therefore, all the blessings of this covenant are secure in Him.

This new covenant in Jesus is no less a healing covenant than the old one. In fact, it is a much better one, for the Healer Himself is now present in us by His Spirit. Therefore, we are more than qualified to choose life and receive healing in Him.

Dear Lord,
  I choose life. I choose blessing. I choose Jesus!
  Thank You, Lord Jesus, for redeeming me from the curse of the Law. I receive

that redemptive work now. Thank You for becoming sin for me, that I might be made the righteousness of God in You. I receive that saving work now. Thank You for the new covenant—the body given for me, the blood shed for me. I receive it now.

Thank You, Lord, that in Jesus Christ I am qualified for every blessing.

Thank You for healing me from the top of my head to the soles of my feet. I receive it now.

In Jesus' name, Amen.

New Testament Healing Scriptures

Praying with Expectation

Ask, and it will be given to you; seek, and you will find; knock, and it will be opened to you. For everyone who asks receives, and he who seeks finds, and to him who knocks it will be opened.

Or what man is there among you who, if his son asks for bread, will give him a stone? Or if he asks for a fish, will he give him a serpent? If you then, being evil, know how to give good gifts to your children, how much more will your Father who is in heaven give good things to those who ask Him! (Matthew 7:7-11)

Ask, seek, knock. Whenever you need anything, go to the Lord for it. Ask boldly. Expect to receive whatever you are asking and find whatever you are seeking. For Jesus said that is exactly what will happen. God will freely open His door to you, for He is a good Father who gives good things to those who ask Him.

The Bible says, "Every good gift and every perfect gift is from above, and comes down from the Father of lights, with whom there is no variation or shadow of turning" (James 1:17). "No good thing will He withhold from those who walk uprightly" (Psalm 84:11).

Ask God for healing, and expect to receive it, for it is a good thing, and He will not withhold it from you.

Dear Lord,

You are a good Father and You give good things to Your children. You are a good Father, and I know that You will not turn me away, but will open Your door to me. So I ask You for healing, knowing that I will receive it. Thank You, Lord.

In Jesus' name, Amen.

Authority for Healing Prayer

Assuredly, I say to you, whatever you bind on earth will be bound in heaven, and whatever you loose on earth will be loosed in heaven. Again I say to you that if two of you agree on earth concerning anything that they ask, it will be done for them by My Father in heaven. For where two or three are gathered together in My name, I am there in the midst of them. (Matthew 18:18-20)

Jesus gives authority to every believer. It is an authority which comes from heaven and is exercised upon the earth. When we exercise this authority, we are actually administering the things of heaven upon the earth.

The basis of this authority is the presence of the Lord Jesus. He promised that when even only two or three are gathered in His name, He is present in our midst. To gather in His name means to be in tune with Him, aligned with His plans and purposes, to act as He would act and ask as He would ask.

The "whatever" and "anything" in this passage includes healing. Therefore, the authority Jesus gives includes the ability to bind sickness, loose the infirmed, agree together for healing—and expect to see it happen. This is a very appropriate exercise of the name of Jesus, because healing has always been an important part of His authority. To the woman with the spirit of infirmity, for example, Jesus declared "Woman, you are loosed from your infirmity" (Luke 13:12).

Asking in Jesus' Name

If you abide in Me, and My words abide in you, you will ask what you desire, and it shall be done for you. (John 15:7)

You did not choose Me, but I chose you and appointed you that you should go and bear fruit, and that your fruit should remain, that whatever you ask the Father in My name He may give you. (John 15:16)

Most assuredly, I say to you, whatever you ask the Father in My name He will give you. Until now you have asked nothing in My name. Ask, and you will receive, that your joy may be full. (John 16:23-24).

Jesus has given us authority to ask in His name. As we abide in Him, we come to know Him more and more, and our hearts become like His heart. As we let His words abide in us and instruct us, our desires are shaped by His desires, and His purposes become ours. We begin to understand who He is and what He wants to do in us and through us. His desire is for us to bear fruit—to live productive lives full of significance and joy.

Asking in the name of Jesus means to ask as He would ask, in harmony with His plans and purposes. When we do, we can know that God hears us, that our desires will be fulfilled, and that we will receive whatever we ask.

The earthly ministry of Jesus reveals that His purpose and will regarding sickness and disease is to heal. He never turned away anyone who came to Him for healing, but the testimony of Scripture is that He healed them all. Therefore, when we ask for healing in the name of Jesus, we can be confident that we will receive it.

Dear Lord,

Teach me to abide in You and to let Your words abide in me. Change my heart until it lines up with Yours. For Your plans for me are good—joy and fruitfulness! I believe that my desire for healing is Your desire, too, for Jesus healed everyone who came to Him for healing. I come now to ask, knowing that I shall receive, for I ask in Jesus' name, Amen.

Exercising Faith

Have faith in God. For assuredly, I say to you, whoever says to this mountain, "Be removed and be cast into the sea," and does not doubt in his heart, but believes that those things he says will be done, he will have whatever he says. Therefore I say to you, whatever things you ask when you pray, believe that you receive them, and you will have them. And whenever you stand praying, if you have anything against anyone, forgive him, that your Father in heaven may also forgive you your trespasses. (Mark 11:22-25)

> What you say is as important as what you believe. Speak to sickness and command it to be removed. Believe that what you say will be done, and you will have what you say.
>
> When you pray for healing, believe you receive it. Believe you receive it at that time and it will be yours.
>
> However, if you have *anything* against *anyone*—forgive. Failure to forgive can be a major impediment to seeing your prayers answered, and whatever can block your prayer can block your healing.

Dear Lord,

I come to You for healing, and in accordance with Your word I believe I receive it now. I command all sickness and disease to leave my body, never to return. If I have anything against anyone, I forgive them now.

In Jesus' name, Amen.

The Faithful, Faith-filled Work of Jesus

The thief does not come except to steal, and to kill, and to destroy. I have come that they may have life, and that they may have it more abundantly. (John 10:10)

Who Himself bore our sins in His own body on the tree, that we, having died to sins, might live for righteousness—by whose stripes you were healed. (1 Peter 2:24)

For this purpose the Son of God was manifested, that He might destroy the works of the devil. (1 John 3:8)

Therefore He is also able to save to the uttermost those who come to God through Him, since He always lives to make intercession for them. (Hebrews 7:25)

Jesus Christ is the same yesterday, today, and forever. (Hebrews 13:8)

> Jesus has come to bring you abundant life. This is not just length of life, not even everlasting life, but it is quality of life, as well. It is the meeting of every

need, with plenty more besides. Jesus bore your sins in His own body on the Cross, and by His stripes you were (and are) healed. He has destroyed all the works of the devil, the thief who comes to steal, kill and destroy.

Jesus is therefore able to completely save those who come to God through Him. The word "save" is *sozo* and means to save, heal, deliver, keep, and make whole. Whatever you need to be saved from, healed of, or delivered from, Jesus is making intercession for you right now. His very presence in heaven at the right hand of God is the assurance of your healing, for the Father will not deny the Son.

Dear Lord Jesus,

Thank You for the abundant life You came to bring to me. Thank You for bearing my sins in Your own body on the Cross. Thank You for destroying all the works of the devil. Thank You for Your continual intercession before the Father for my healing.

Jesus, You are the same yesterday, today, and forever. What You did in Your earthly ministry, You are still doing today. In agreement with Your word, I declare that by Your stripes I am healed.

Amen.

The Goodness of God Toward us

What then shall we say to these things? If God is for us, who can be against us? He who did not spare His own Son, but delivered Him up for us all, how shall He not with Him also freely give us all things? Who shall bring a charge against God's elect? It is God who justifies. Who is he who condemns? It is Christ who died, and furthermore is also risen, who is even at the right hand of God, who also makes intercession for us. Who shall separate us from the love of Christ? Shall tribulation, or distress, or persecution, or famine, or nakedness, or peril, or sword? ... Yet in all these things we are more than conquerors through Him who loved us. For I am persuaded that neither death nor life, nor angels nor principalities nor powers, nor things present nor things to come, nor height nor depth, nor any other created thing, shall be able to separate us from the love of God which is in Christ Jesus our Lord. (Romans 8:31-39)

All the promises of God in Him are Yes, and in Him Amen, to the glory of God through us. (2 Corinthians 1:20)

Be anxious for nothing, but in everything by prayer and supplication, with thanksgiving, let your requests be made known to God; and the peace of God, which surpasses all understanding, will guard your hearts and minds through Christ Jesus. (Philippians 4:6-7)

For God has not given us a spirit of fear, but of power and of love and of a sound mind. (2 Timothy 1:7)

Every good gift and every perfect gift is from above, and comes down from the Father of lights, with whom there is no variation or shadow of turning. (James 1:17)

His divine power has given to us all things that pertain to life and godliness, through the knowledge of Him who called us by glory and virtue, by which have been given to us exceedingly great and precious promises, that through these you may be partakers of the divine nature, having escaped the corruption that is in the world through lust. (2 Peter 1:3-4)

> There is no corruption in the divine nature—no sickness, no disease, no lack, no poverty. In the divine nature, there is health, wholeness and prosperity. The promise of God is that we can partake of His divine nature, by His divine power.

Dear Lord,

I thank you that nothing can separate me from the love You have for me in Christ Jesus, and that all Your promises in Him are "Yes" and "Amen." Thank You for the peace You bring to my heart and mind, the wholeness of knowing that I am made complete in Jesus. Every good gift comes from You, and You never change.

Thank You, Lord, for the Holy Spirit, who gives me power and love and a sound mind. Your divine power has given me everything I need for life and godliness. Thank You for my healing.

In Jesus' name, Amen.

Faith

Faith comes by hearing, and hearing by the word of God. (Romans 10:17)

Now faith is the substance of things hoped for, the evidence of things not seen. (Hebrews 11:1)

Without faith it is impossible to please Him, for he who comes to God must believe that He is, and that He is a rewarder of those who diligently seek Him. (Hebrews 11:6)

This is the victory that has overcome the world—our faith. (1 John 5.4)

Faith pleases God! Faith is believing what God says, and that pleases Him. As we listen to His Word, the Holy Spirit makes faith come alive in our hearts.

Faith is active. To exercise faith is to diligently seek after God, agreeing with His Word, and saying what He says. This is how we receive the promises in His Word.

Faith is substance. The Greek word for "substance" is *hypostasis*. It is the underlying reality of a thing. Sometimes this word was used to refer to a title-deed to a piece of land. When you possess the title-deed to a thing, you know that thing is yours. You have a positive expectation, a joyful anticipation, that you are going to see that thing and enjoy its benefits—this is what the Greek word for "hope" means. We might say it this way: Faith is the title-deed, the underlying reality of what we are joyfully anticipating and fully expecting to see.

In the matter of sickness and disease, faith is believing what God has said about healing. For example, "By His stripes we are healed" (Isaiah 53:5). As we believe that Word, we possess the underlying reality of our healing, and we can expect to see it happen.

Faith is the victory that overcomes sickness. In the healing stories of Jesus, He often said to those who were healed, "Your faith has made you well." Faith for healing is believing and receiving the victory Jesus has won over sin and death.

Dear Lord,

Thank You for Your Word, which causes faith to arise within me. I will exercise this faith and seek after You with all my heart, knowing that it pleases You. By faith, I receive the victory Jesus won for me over sin and death. By faith, I possess the title-deed to my healing and I wait with joyful expectation for it to appear.

In Jesus' name, Amen.

Redeemed from the Curse

Christ has redeemed us from the curse of the law, having become a curse for us (for it is written, "Cursed is everyone who hangs on a tree"), that the blessing of Abraham might come upon the Gentiles in Christ Jesus. (Galatians 3:13-14)

Christ has redeemed us from *every* curse of the Law. We find a list of these curses in Deuteronomy 28:15-68, which includes: plague, consumption, fever, inflammation, severe burning fever, tumors, scab, "the itch," madness, blindness, confusion of heart, severe boils on knees and legs (from the soles of the feet to the top of the head), extraordinary plagues, great and prolonged plagues, serious and prolonged sickness, all the diseases of Egypt. Verse 61 tells us that the curse also includes every plague and sickness not specifically mentioned by name.

Jesus redeemed us from the curse by becoming a curse for us. By His death on the Cross He cancelled every aspect of the curse. Sickness, disease, malady and pain have no right to come upon us. What is more, Jesus has freed us to receive every benefit and blessing God promised Abraham (represented in Deuteronomy 28:1-14).

Dear Lord,

I thank You that Jesus took my place on the Cross and became a curse for me. Thank You that He has redeemed me from every sickness, disease, malady and pain. Thank You for including me in every benefit and blessing of Abraham, which includes healing and wholeness.

In Jesus' name, Amen.

The Holy Spirit Dwelling in Us

But if the Spirit of Him who raised Jesus from the dead dwells in you, He who raised Christ from the dead will also give life to your mortal bodies through His Spirit who dwells in you. (Romans 8:11)

The Spirit of God, whose power raised the Lord Jesus Christ from the dead, is also at work in us. His power is now present in us and is able to bring life and health to our bodies today.

Dear Lord,

Thank You for the Holy Spirit dwelling in me, and for Your great power at work in me, which is more than able to heal my body of all sickness and disease. I receive it now.

In Jesus' name, Amen.

Spiritual Warfare and Healing Prayer

Thanks be to God, who gives us the victory through our Lord Jesus Christ. (1 Corinthians 15:57)

For the weapons of our warfare are not carnal but mighty in God for pulling down strongholds, casting down arguments and every high thing that exalts itself against the knowledge of God, bringing every thought into captivity to the obedience of Christ. (2 Corinthians 10:4-5)

Finally, be strong in the Lord and in his mighty power. Put on the full armor of God so that you can take your stand against the devil's schemes. For our struggle is not against flesh and blood, but against the rulers, against the authorities, against the powers of this dark world and against the spiritual forces of evil in the heavenly realms. Therefore put on the full armor of God, so that when the day of evil comes, you may be able to stand your ground, and after you have done everything, to stand. Stand firm then, with the belt of truth buckled around your waist, with the breastplate of righteousness in place, and with your feet fitted with the readiness that comes from the gospel of peace. In addition to all this, take up the shield of faith, with which you can extinguish all the flaming arrows of the evil one. Take the helmet of salvation and the sword of the Spirit, which is the word of God. And pray in the Spirit on all occasions with all kinds of prayers and requests. (Ephesians 6:10-18 *NIV*)

 When the devil tries to bring sickness against you, bring every thought of it into captivity, making it subject to the lordship of Christ, who is our healer. Prepare to stand your ground for healing by putting on the full armor of God:

- The belt of truth is a person. Jesus said, "I am the way, the truth, and the life" (John 14:6). He encompasses our whole life and being.
- The breastplate of righteousness is Christ, who is our righteousness.

- ✤ The gospel of peace is the wholeness we have in Christ. We stand in His completeness.
- ✤ The shield of faith extinguishes every lie and slander the devil brings against us. We believe the Word of God, not the deceptions of the enemy.
- ✤ The helmet of salvation is the full covering of God's work in us. The Greek word for "salvation" refers to deliverance, preservation, wholeness and healing.
- ✤ The sword of the Spirit is the Word of God. It is the weapon we use to attack sickness and disease. Jesus is the *living* Word of God. By His name and in His blood we have the victory.

Pray at all times with all kinds of prayers, as the Spirit leads. Prayer is the means by which we apply all the elements of our spiritual armor.

You are of God, little children, and have overcome them, because He who is in you is greater than he who is in the world. (1 John 4:4)

Dear Lord,

Today I bring every thought of sickness and disease captive to You.

Today I put on the Lord Jesus Christ, who is the truth which surrounds me, the breastplate of righteousness which protects me, the peace and wholeness in which I stand, and my helmet of victory. He is my Savior, my Deliverer, my Healer.

Today I hold out the shield of faith to disarm every lie and attack of the devil, and I speak the truth of the Word of God over every situation in my life.

Today I will pray at all times with all kinds of prayer, as the Holy Spirit leads.

Today I will give thanks to You for the victory, for greater is He that is in me than he that is in the world.

Thank You for my healing.

In Jesus' name, Amen.

The Prayer of faith

Is anyone among you sick? Let him call for the elders of the church, and let them pray over him, anointing him with oil in the name of the Lord. And the prayer of faith will save the sick, and the Lord will raise him up. And if he has committed sins, he will be forgiven. (James 5:14-15)

Ask in faith, with no doubting, for he who doubts is like a wave of the sea driven and tossed by the wind. For let not that man suppose that he will receive anything from the Lord. (James 1:6-7)

> Prayer for healing is not about overcoming God's reluctance, for God is not at all reluctant to heal. Prayer for healing is about laying hold of God's willingness to heal. It is about applying the provision He has already made for healing in the work of Jesus.
>
> Ask in faith. The Bible says that the prayer of faith will save the sick, that is, make them well. The prayer of faith is not about *begging* God, it is about *believing* God. Begging is doubting God's desire to heal. Believing is taking God at His word.
>
> It is like cashing a check. We do not take a check to the bank on which it is drawn and beg them to give us the money. We simply present the check and expect to receive what has already been promised to us by the writer of the check. It is the same way with the prayer of faith. Do not waver between praying and begging for what God has already promised. Begging and doubting have no guarantee of receiving anything from God, but God's Word affirms that the prayer of faith will heal the sick.

Dear Lord,

Thank You for forgiving my sin. I receive it now by faith. Thank You also for the provision You have made for my healing. I apply it now by faith.

In Jesus' name, Amen.

Confidence in God

Beloved, if our heart does not condemn us, we have confidence toward God. And whatever we ask we receive from Him, because we keep His commandments and do those things that are pleasing in His sight. And this is His commandment: that we should believe on the name of His Son Jesus Christ and love one another, as He gave us commandment. (1 John 3:21-23)

> Faith pleases God, and so does love, for God is love (1 John 4:16). When we believe in the Lord Jesus Christ, and have love for one another, we may confidently come before Him and ask for healing, knowing that we will receive it.

Now this is the confidence that we have in Him, that if we ask anything according to His will, He hears us. And if we know that He hears us, whatever we ask, we know that we have the petitions that we have asked of Him. (1 John 5:14-15)

> We can know the will of God by believing the Word of God. The Scriptures listed in this book demonstrate that God's will and desire is to heal. Therefore, we can come confidently before Him and ask for healing— knowing that He hears us and that we have what we have asked of him.

Let us hold fast the confession of our hope without wavering, for He who promised is faithful. (Hebrews 10:23)

Therefore do not cast away your confidence, which has great reward. For you have need of endurance, so that after you have done the will of God, you may receive the promise. (Hebrews 10:35-36)

Dear Lord,

I hold on to the promises of Your Word, for You are faithful. I come in the name of Jesus Christ, asking for healing according to Your will, confident that I shall see it manifest. Thank You.

In Jesus' name, Amen.

Spirit, Soul and Body

Now may the God of peace Himself sanctify you completely; and may your whole spirit, soul, and body be preserved blameless at the coming of our Lord Jesus Christ. He who calls you is faithful, who also will do it. (1 Thessalonians 5:23-24)

> The Greek word for "preserve" is *tereo* and means to guard, or keep from loss, injury or harm. This applies to the body as well as to the spirit and the soul. God's purpose is to present us complete—spirit, soul and body.

Beloved, I pray that you may prosper in all things and be in health, just as your soul prospers. (3 John 2)

How is your soul prospering? Is there something you need to repent of, confess and receive cleansing for? "If we confess our sins, He is faithful and just to forgive us our sins and to cleanse us from all unrighteousness" (1 John 1:9).

Is there someone you need to forgive? "Whenever you stand praying, if you have anything against anyone, forgive him, that your Father in heaven may also forgive you your trespasses" (Mark 11:25).

Are you seeking the rule and reign of God, and His way of being and doing right? "But seek first the kingdom of God and His righteousness, and all these things shall be added to you" (Matthew 6:33).

Dear Lord,

I thank You that You care for my whole being—spirit, soul and body—and that You desire for me to prosper in all things. I know that I will be preserved blameless and without fault at the coming of the Lord Jesus Christ, for You are faithful. I receive Your health and prosperity now, trusting in Your Word.

In Jesus' name, Amen.

The Healing Ministry of Jesus

The healing ministry of Jesus demonstrates that it is God's desire and will to heal. When Jesus healed, He was in perfect harmony with the Fahter and the Spirit. Preaching to Cornelius, Peter declared that "God anointed Jesus of Nazareth with the Holy Spirit and with power, who went about doing good and healing all who were oppressed by the devil, for God was with Him" (Acts 10:38).

We also see the testimony of Jesus Himself, that everything He did was according to the Father's will and pleasure:

> Then Jesus answered and said to them, "Most assuredly, I say to you, the Son can do nothing of Himself, but what He sees the Father do; for whatever He does, the Son also does in like manner." (John 5:19)

> "I can of Myself do nothing. As I hear, I judge; and My judgment is righteous, because I do not seek My own will but the will of the Father who sent Me." (John 5:30)

> Then Jesus said to them, "When you lift up the Son of Man, then you will know that I am He, and that I do nothing of Myself; but as My Father taught Me, I speak these things. And He who sent Me is with Me. The Father has not left Me alone, for I always do those things that please Him." (John 8:28-29)

In the healing stories of Jesus, we see that He is very accessible to those who desire healing. He is easy to entreat, easy to receive from. We also see that Jesus never turned away anyone who came to Him, or was brought to Him, for healing. The repeated testimony of Scripture is that "Jesus healed them all.

The Jesus who heals in these stories is the same Jesus today. He is still in the healing business. He is still easy to entreat, and He will not turn away anyone who comes to Him for healing. "Jesus Christ is the same, yesterday, today and forever" (Hebrews 13:8).

As you read and meditate on these healing accounts, pay close attention to the dynamics of faith and divine power at work. Observe when and how and by whom faith is released (that is, activated or exercised), and how that faith brings forth the healing power of God.

Jesus is Anointed for Healing Ministry

So He came to Nazareth, where He had been brought up. And as His custom was, He went into the synagogue on the Sabbath day, and stood up to read. And He was handed the book of the prophet Isaiah. And when He had opened the book, He found the place where it was written:

"The Spirit of the LORD is upon Me, because He has anointed Me to preach the gospel to the poor; He has sent Me to heal the brokenhearted, to proclaim liberty to the captives and recovery of sight to the blind, to set at liberty those who are oppressed; to proclaim the acceptable year of the LORD."*

Then He closed the book, and gave it back to the attendant and sat down. And the eyes of all who were in the synagogue were fixed on Him. And He began to say to them, "Today this Scripture is fulfilled in your hearing." (Luke 4:16-21)

* The NIV has "to proclaim the year of the Lord's favor."

Release of Faith: Jesus declared, "Today this Scripture is fulfilled in your hearing."

Dear Lord,

I believe that You anointed Jesus to bring good news to the poor, to heal the brokenhearted, to free the captive and oppressed, to give sight to the blind, and to proclaim that now is the time for the favor of the Lord.

Today this Scripture is fulfilled in my hearing, and I receive Your healing touch. Thank You, Lord.

In Jesus' name, Amen.

Jesus Heals a Leper

When He had come down from the mountain, great multitudes followed Him. And behold, a leper came and worshiped Him, saying, "Lord, if You are willing, You can make me clean." Then Jesus put out His hand and touched him, saying, "I am willing; be cleansed." Immediately his leprosy was cleansed. (Matthew 8:1-3; see also Mark 1:40-42 and Luke 5:12-15)

Mark adds that Jesus was "moved with compassion."

Release of Faith:

- The man said, "If You are willing, You can make me clean."
- Jesus answered, "I am willing: be cleansed."
- Jesus laid His hands on the man.

Dear Lord,

I thank You that You are moved with compassion, and that the only time You were ever asked if You were willing to heal, the answer was Yes. Lord, I believe that Your answer still is Yes, and so I come to You. Thank You for Your healing touch.

In Jesus' name, Amen.

Jesus Heals the Centurion's Servant

Now when Jesus had entered Capernaum, a centurion came to Him, pleading with Him, saying, "Lord, my servant is lying at home paralyzed, dreadfully tormented." And Jesus said to him, "I will come and heal him." The centurion answered and said, "Lord, I am not worthy that You should come under my roof. But only speak a word, and my servant will be healed. For I also am a man under authority, having soldiers under me. And I say to this one, 'Go,' and he goes; and to another, 'Come,' and he comes; and to my servant, 'Do this,' and he does it." When Jesus heard it, He marveled, and said to those who followed, "Assuredly, I say to you, I have not found such great faith, not even in Israel! ... Then Jesus said to the centurion, "Go your way; and as you have believed, so let it be done for you." And his servant was healed that same hour. (Matthew 8:5-10, 13: see also Luke 7:1-10)

> The centurion understood the authority of Jesus and had complete faith in His right to exercise it. He knew that a word of healing from the lips of Jesus would be quite sufficient to heal his servant. Psalm107:20 says, "He sent His word and healed them."
>
> Release of Faith:
>
> ✣ The centurion said, "Speak a word, and my servant will be healed."
> ✣ Jesus answered, "Go your way; and as you have believed, so let it be done for you."

Dear Lord,

One word from You is sufficient to heal me. I believe that You send that healing word, and I receive it now. Thank You, Lord.

In Jesus' name, Amen.

Jesus Heals Peter's Mother-in-Law

Now when Jesus had come into Peter's house, He saw his wife's mother lying sick with a fever. So He touched her hand, and the fever left her. And she arose and served them.

When evening had come, they brought to Him many who were demon-possessed. And He cast out the spirits with a word, and healed all who were sick, that it might be fulfilled which was spoken by Isaiah the prophet, saying: "He Himself took our infirmities and bore our sicknesses." (Matthew 8:14-17)

So He stood over her and rebuked the fever, and it left her. And immediately she arose and served them. When the sun was setting, all those who had any that were sick with various diseases brought them to Him; and He laid His hands on every one of them and healed them. And demons also came out of many, crying out and saying, "You are the Christ, the Son of God!" (Luke 4:39-41)

Jesus ministered healing to Peter's mother-in-law by a combination of His gentle touch and commanding authority.

Matthew and Luke both note that Jesus healed *all* the sick who came or were brought to him for healing. None were turned away, and all received from Him.

Release of Faith:

- Jesus laid hands on Peter's mother-in-law.
- Jesus rebuked the fever.
- The sick and demonized were brought to Jesus.
- Jesus cast out the demonic spirits with a word.
- Jesus laid hands on every one of the sick, and they were healed.

Dear Lord Jesus,

Thank You for taking my infirmities and bearing my sicknesses. Your gentle touch raises me up, and the voice of Your command sets me free. By Your stripes I am healed.

In Jesus' name, Amen.

Jesus Heals a Paralytic

Now it happened on a certain day, as He was teaching, that there were Pharisees and teachers of the law sitting by, who had come out of every town of Galilee, Judea, and Jerusalem. And the power of the Lord was present to heal them.

Then behold, men brought on a bed a man who was paralyzed, whom they sought to bring in and lay before Him. And when they could not find how they might bring him in, because of the crowd, they went up on the housetop and let him down with his bed through the tiling into the midst before Jesus.

When He saw their faith, He said to him, "Man, your sins are forgiven you."

And the scribes and the Pharisees began to reason, saying, "Who is this who speaks blasphemies? Who can forgive sins but God alone?"

But when Jesus perceived their thoughts, He answered and said to them, "Why are you reasoning in your hearts? Which is easier, to say, 'Your sins are forgiven you,' or to say, 'Rise up and walk'? But that you may know that the Son of Man has power on earth to forgive sins"—He said to the man who was paralyzed, "I say to you, arise, take up your bed, and go to your house."

Immediately he rose up before them, took up what he had been lying on, and departed to his own house, glorifying God. And they were all amazed, and they glorified God and were filled with fear, saying, "We have seen strange things today!" (Luke 5:17-26)

> Psalm 103 says, "Bless the LORD, O my soul and forget not all His benefits: Who forgives all your iniquities, Who heals all your diseases" (v. 2-3). Isaiah 53 says that Jesus bore our sicknesses as well as our sins. These two—sin and sickness—go together. Death entered the world because of sin (Romans 5:12), and sickness is but an intermediate form of death.
>
> By His death on the Cross, Jesus has authority both to forgive sins and heal diseases, but the forgiveness of sins is the greater authority. Jesus was free to heal the man of his paralytic condition because He had authority to forgive the man of his sins. The authority for both is based on the atoning work of Jesus on the Cross. Sin is no longer an impediment to healing because Jesus died to forgive us our sins.
>
> Release of Faith:
>
> ❧ The man's friends let him down through the roof, into the presence of Jesus. This act released faith, for the Bible says, "When He *saw* their faith."
> ❧ Jesus said, "Your sins are forgiven," and then said, "Arise, take up your bed."
> ❧ The man did what he could not do before. He arose, took up his bed, and departed to his house.

Dear Lord,
> *Thank You for forgiving all my sins. Thank You for healing all my diseases.*
> *In Jesus' name, Amen.*

Jesus Heals Jairus' Daughter and a Woman with a Flow of Blood

So it was, when Jesus returned, that the multitude welcomed Him, for they were all waiting for Him. And behold, there came a man named Jairus, and he was a ruler of the synagogue. And he fell down at Jesus' feet and begged Him to come to his house, for he had an only daughter about twelve years of age, and she was dying. But as He went, the multitudes thronged Him.

Now a woman, having a flow of blood for twelve years, who had spent all her livelihood on physicians and could not be healed by any, came from behind and touched the border of His garment. And immediately her flow of blood stopped.

And Jesus said, "Who touched Me?"

When all denied it, Peter and those with him said, "Master, the multitudes throng and press You, and You say, 'Who touched Me?'"

But Jesus said, "Somebody touched Me, for I perceived power going out from Me."

Now when the woman saw that she was not hidden, she came trembling; and falling down before Him, she declared to Him in the presence of all the people the reason she had touched Him and how she was healed immediately.

And He said to her, "Daughter, be of good cheer; your faith has made you well. Go in peace."

While He was still speaking, someone came from the ruler of the synagogue's house, saying to him, "Your daughter is dead. Do not trouble the Teacher."

But when Jesus heard it, He answered him, saying, "Do not be afraid; only believe, and she will be made well."

When He came into the house, He permitted no one to go in except Peter, James, and John, and the father and mother of the girl. Now all wept and mourned for her; but He said, "Do not weep; she is not dead, but sleeping."

And they ridiculed Him, knowing that she was dead. But He put them all outside, took her by the hand and called, saying, "Little girl, arise."

Then her spirit returned, and she arose immediately. And He commanded that she be given something to eat. And her parents were astonished, but He charged them to tell no one what had happened. (Luke 8:40-56; see also Matthew 9:18-26 and Mark 5:21-43)

Concerning the woman with the flow of blood, Matthew's account adds: "For she said to herself, 'If only I may touch His garment, I shall be made well'" (Matthew 9:21).

Release of Faith:

ᑫ Jairus came to Jesus, asking Him to come to His house, with the expectation that his daughter would be healed.

- The woman with the flow of blood said, "If I touch His garment, I shall be made well.
- The woman touched the hem of Jesus' garment in faith.
- When Jairus' servants brought news of his daughter's death, Jesus told him, "Do not be afraid; only believe, and she will be made well."
- Jairus obeyed, for he continued bringing Jesus to his daughter.
- Jesus said, "Do not weep; she is not dead, but sleeping." Then He eliminated all unbelief from the room by removing those who ridiculed.
- Jesus laid hands on the girl and said, "Little girl, arise."

Notice also the dynamics of power in this story:

- The woman experienced the power of Jesus in a very tangible way, for she immediately knew she was healed.
- Jesus experienced power going out from Him in a very tangible way, and immediately knew that it was drawn out by faith.
- The garment of Jesus was a conduit of power. For power went out from Jesus, through the hem of His garment, and into the woman.
- This same power was great enough to heal a long-term affliction and bring a little girl back to life.

Dear Lord Jesus,

I thank You that You are easy to entreat, that You honor faith, and that You do not let us lose hope. I will believe only, and I will not contaminate my faith with fear. Thank You for Your healing power. I receive it now.

In Jesus' name, Amen.

Many Others Touch Jesus' Garment and are Healed

When they had crossed over, they came to the land of Gennesaret. And when the men of that place recognized Him, they sent out into all that surrounding region, brought to Him all who were sick, and begged Him that they might only touch the hem of His garment. And as many as touched it were made perfectly well. (Matthew 14:34-36; see also Mark 6:53-56)

Here again is the dynamic of power tangibly transferred through something as simple as a garment, and drawn out by faith. Notice also that as many as touched the hem of His garment were made well. Jesus healed them all.

Release of Faith: All those who touched the hem of Jesus' garment were healed.

Jesus Heals Two Blind Men (see Matthew 20:29-34)

When Jesus departed from there, two blind men followed Him, crying out and saying, "Son of David, have mercy on us!" And when He had come into the house, the blind men came to Him.
And Jesus said to them, "Do you believe that I am able to do this?"
They said to Him, "Yes, Lord."
Then He touched their eyes, saying, "According to your faith let it be to you." And their eyes were opened. (Matthew 9:27-30)

Release of Faith:

- When Jesus asked them, "Do you believe I am able to do this?" they answered, "Yes, Lord."
- Jesus touched their eyes and said, "According to your faith let it be to you."

Dear Lord,
   I believe that You are both willing and able to heal me, and I release my faith now to receive it.

In Jesus' name, Amen.

Jesus Heals a Man who was Mute and Demonized

As they went out, behold, they brought to Him a man, mute and demon-possessed. And when the demon was cast out, the mute spoke. And the multitudes marveled, saying, "It was never seen like this in Israel!" (Matthew 9:32-33)

Many times, we find that an affliction is the result of a demonic influence. But

Jesus has authority to cast out demons. He was anointed by God to proclaim freedom for the captives, and to set at liberty those who are oppressed. ✳Believers also have been given authority to cast out demons in His name.

Release of Faith:

- Bringing the man to Jesus for healing was a release of faith.
- Jesus exercised power and authority to cast out the demon.
- The man who was mute opened his mouth and spoke.

Jesus Heals a Man with a Withered Hand on the Sabbath

Now it happened on another Sabbath, also, that He entered the synagogue and taught. And a man was there whose right hand was withered. So the scribes and Pharisees watched Him closely, whether He would heal on the Sabbath, that they might find an accusation against Him.

But He knew their thoughts, and said to the man who had the withered hand, "Arise and stand here."

And he arose and stood.

Then Jesus said to them, "I will ask you one thing: Is it lawful on the Sabbath to do good or to do evil, to save life or to destroy?"

And when He had looked around at them all, He said to the man, "Stretch out your hand."

And he did so, and his hand was restored as whole as the other. (Luke 6:6-10; see also Matthew 12:9-13 and Mark 3:1-5)

The right hand, particularly, represented honor and strength. To restore the man's hand would restore the honor and strength of His life. Jesus demonstrated that it is always lawful to do good and heal. In fact, it would be evil to not heal. By this, Jesus reveals that it is God's will to heal, for God is not evil.

Release of Faith:

- Jesus said, "Stretch out your hand."
- The man did what he could not do before and stretched out his hand.

Dear Lord,
  Thank You for Your healing word.

In Jesus' name, Amen.

Jesus Heals a Man with Dropsy on the Sabbath

Now it happened, as He went into the house of one of the rulers of the Pharisees to eat bread on the Sabbath, that they watched Him closely. And behold, there was a certain man before Him who had dropsy.*

And Jesus, answering, spoke to the lawyers and Pharisees, saying, "Is it lawful to heal on the Sabbath?"

But they kept silent. And He took him and healed him, and let him go. (Luke 14:1-4)

Release of Faith: Jesus laid hands on the man and healed him.

Dear Lord,
  Thank You for Your healing touch.

In Jesus name, Amen.

Jesus Heals the Daughter of a Canaanite Woman

Then Jesus went out from there and departed to the region of Tyre and Sidon. And behold, a woman of Canaan came from that region and cried out to Him, saying, "Have mercy on me, O Lord, Son of David! My daughter is severely demon-possessed."

But He answered her not a word. And His disciples came and urged Him, saying, "Send her away, for she cries out after us."

But He answered and said, "I was not sent except to the lost sheep of the house of Israel."

Then she came and worshiped Him, saying, "Lord, help me!"

But He answered and said, "It is not good to take the children's bread and throw it to the little dogs."

And she said, "Yes, Lord, yet even the little dogs eat the crumbs which fall from their masters' table."

Then Jesus answered and said to her, "O woman, great is your faith! Let it be to you as you desire."

And her daughter was healed from that very hour. (Matthew 15:21-28)

Healing is the "children's bread." That is, it belongs to the children of God's household. God is a good Father, and will not withhold the bread of healing from you. Notice also that this healing was a deliverance from demonization.

Release of Faith:

- ☙ The woman came to Jesus for mercy.
- ☙ The woman would not be turned away, but continued to call on Jesus for mercy.
- ☙ The woman expressed that even a little "crumb" would be sufficient to completely meet her need.
- ☙ Jesus answered, "O woman, great is your faith! Let it be to you as you desire."

Dear Lord,

You are a good Father, and I thank You that You do not deny Your children the bread of healing. Just one word, just one touch, is more than enough to heal every sickness and disease. I release my faith now to receive healing.

In Jesus' name, Amen.

Jesus Heals When the Disciples Couldn't

And when they had come to the multitude, a man came to Him, kneeling down to Him and saying, "Lord, have mercy on my son, for he is an epileptic and suffers severely; for he often falls into the fire and often into the water. So I brought him to Your disciples, but they could not cure him."

Then Jesus answered and said, "O faithless and perverse generation, how long shall I be with you? How long shall I bear with you? Bring him here to Me." And Jesus rebuked the demon, and it came out of him; and the child was cured from that very hour.

Then the disciples came to Jesus privately and said, "Why could we not cast it out?"

So Jesus said to them, "Because of your unbelief; for assuredly, I say to you, if you have faith as a mustard seed, you will say to this mountain, 'Move from here to there,' and it will move; and nothing will be impossible for you. However, this kind does not go out except by prayer and fasting." (Matthew 17:14-21)

Mark's account adds:

So He asked his father, "How long has this been happening to him?"

And he said, "From childhood. And often he has thrown him both into the fire and into the water to destroy him. But if You can do anything, have compassion on us and help us."

Jesus said to him, "If you can believe, all things are possible to him who believes."

Immediately the father of the child cried out and said with tears, "Lord, I believe; help my unbelief!"

When Jesus saw that the people came running together, He rebuked the unclean spirit, saying to it, "Deaf and dumb spirit, I command you, come out of him and enter him no more!"

Then the spirit cried out, convulsed him greatly, and came out of him. And he became as one dead, so that many said, "He is dead." But Jesus took him by the hand and lifted him up, and he arose. (Mark 9:21-27; see also Luke 9:37-42)

Release of Faith:

- ∾ The man brought his son to Jesus.
- ∾ Jesus taught about releasing faith when He said, "If you have faith as a mustard seed, you will *say* to this mountain, 'Move from here to there,' and it will move." One way faith is released is by *saying*.
- ∾ The man declared his faith and asked Jesus to do something about his unbelief. He was determined to exercise faith only, refusing to act or speak in unbelief.
- ∾ Jesus exercised power and authority when He rebuked the demon, commanding it to come out and stay out.

Dear Lord,

I release faith now and speak Your healing Word over my life. Help me not to speak or act contrary to Your promise, for all things are possible to those who exercise faith. Thank You for Your healing power. I receive it now.

In Jesus' name, Amen.

Jesus Heals Two Blind Men (see Matthew 9:27-30)

Now as they went out of Jericho, a great multitude followed Him. And behold, two blind men sitting by the road, when they heard that Jesus was passing by, cried out, saying, "Have mercy on us, O Lord, Son of David!" Then the multitude warned them that they should be quiet; but they cried out all the more, saying, "Have mercy on us, O Lord, Son of David!"

So Jesus stood still and called them, and said, "What do you want Me to do for you?"

They said to Him, "Lord, that our eyes may be opened."

So Jesus had compassion and touched their eyes. And immediately their eyes received sight, and they followed Him. (Matthew 20:29-34)

Release of Faith:

- The blind men cried out to Jesus for mercy
- When Jesus asked what they wanted Him to do for them, they answered, "Lord, that our eyes may be opened."
- Jesus touched their eyes and they received their sight.

Dear Lord,

I want to be healed. Thank You for Your compassionate heart and for being so accessible to my need. I receive Your healing touch now.

In Jesus' name, Amen.

Jesus Heals Blind Bartimaeus
(see above, *Jesus Heals Two Blind Men*)

Now they came to Jericho. As He went out of Jericho with His disciples and a great multitude, blind Bartimaeus, the son of Timaeus, sat by the road begging. And when he heard that it was Jesus of Nazareth, he began to cry out and say, "Jesus, Son of David, have mercy on me!" Then many warned him to be quiet; but he cried out all the more, "Son of David, have mercy on me!"

So Jesus stood still and commanded him to be called. Then they called the blind man, saying to him, "Be of good cheer. Rise, He is calling you." And throwing aside his garment, he rose and came to Jesus.

So Jesus answered and said to him, "What do you want Me to do for you?"

74

The blind man said to Him, "Rabboni, that I may receive my sight."

Then Jesus said to him, "Go your way; your faith has made you well." And immediately he received his sight and followed Jesus on the road. (Mark 10:46-52; see also Matthew 20:29-34 and Luke 18:35-43)

This is Mark's account of the story above (see *Jesus heals two blind men*). It is included here because of the additional faith dynamics it presents.

Release of Faith:

- Bartimaeus cried out to Jesus for mercy.
- Though others tried to quiet him, Bartimaeus continued to cry out even louder. Faith persists.
- When Jesus called him over, Bartimaeus cast aside his beggar's robe and went to Jesus. By faith, he knew he would no longer be a beggar.
- When Jesus asked him what he wanted, Bartimaeus answered, "That I may receive my sight." Faith is specific to the need.
- Jesus said, "Go your way; your faith has made you well." Faith lays hold of the healing power of God.
- Bartimaeus received his sight and followed Jesus.

Jesus Heals a Man who was Deaf and Mute

Again, departing from the region of Tyre and Sidon, He came through the midst of the region of Decapolis to the Sea of Galilee. Then they brought to Him one who was deaf and had an impediment in his speech, and they begged Him to put His hand on him. And He took him aside from the multitude, and put His fingers in his ears, and He spat and touched his tongue.

Then, looking up to heaven, He sighed, and said to him, "Ephphatha," that is, "Be opened."

Immediately his ears were opened, and the impediment of his tongue was loosed, and he spoke plainly. Then He commanded them that they should tell no one; but the more He commanded them, the more widely they proclaimed it. And they were astonished beyond measure, saying, "He has done all things well. He makes both the deaf to hear and the mute to speak." (Mark 7:31-37)

Release of Faith:

- ❧ They brought the deaf and mute man for Jesus to lay hands on him.
- ❧ Jesus laid hands on him.
- ❧ Jesus said to him, "Be opened," and his ears were opened and his tongue was loosed.

Jesus Heals a Blind Man

Then He came to Bethsaida; and they brought a blind man to Him, and begged Him to touch him. So He took the blind man by the hand and led him out of the town. And when He had spit on his eyes and put His hands on him, He asked him if he saw anything.

And he looked up and said, "I see men like trees, walking."

Then He put His hands on his eyes again and made him look up. And he was restored and saw everyone clearly. (Mark 8:22-25)

Release of Faith:

- ❧ They brought a blind man for Jesus to lay hands on him.
- ❧ Jesus laid hands on him.
- ❧ Jesus laid hands on him a second time. He did not settle for a partial healing, but expected a full and complete healing.

Dear Lord,

You give sight to the blind, hearing to the deaf, speech to the speechless. Thank You for Your power to break all curses and free me from all demonic oppression. I believe Your Word and receive Your healing touch now.

In Jesus' name, Amen.

Jesus Heals a Woman who had a Spirit of Infirmity

Now He was teaching in one of the synagogues on the Sabbath. And behold, there was a woman who had a spirit of infirmity eighteen years, and was bent over and could in no way raise herself up.

But when Jesus saw her, He called her to Him and said to her, "Woman, you are loosed from your infirmity." And He laid His hands on her, and immediately she was made straight, and glorified God.

But the ruler of the synagogue answered with indignation, because Jesus had healed on the Sabbath; and he said to the crowd, "There are six days on which men ought to work; therefore come and be healed on them, and not on the Sabbath day."

The Lord then answered him and said, "Hypocrite! Does not each one of you on the Sabbath loose his ox or donkey from the stall, and lead it away to water it? So ought not this woman, being a daughter of Abraham, whom Satan has bound— think of it—for eighteen years, be loosed from this bond on the Sabbath?"

And when He said these things, all His adversaries were put to shame; and all the multitude rejoiced for all the glorious things that were done by Him. (Luke 13:10-17)

Jesus said, "Ought not this woman, being a daughter of Abraham ... be loosed?" The word "ought" shows, not only the appropriateness of healing God's people, it demonstrates the obligation to heal God's people.

This woman had a right to receive healing because she was a "daughter of Abraham," and therefore an heir to the covenant promises God made to Abraham. We, also, are heirs to those same promises. The Bible says, "And if you are Christ's, then you are Abraham's seed, and heirs according to the promise" (Galatians 3:29). This means that we, also, have a covenant right to receive healing.

Jesus "loosed" the woman from her infirmity. He has given believers that same authority to bind and to loose: "Assuredly, I say to you, whatever you bind on earth will be bound in heaven, and whatever you loose on earth will be loosed in heaven" (Matthew 18:18).

Release of Faith:

- ❧ Jesus claimed covenantal blessing on the woman's behalf.
- ❧ Jesus said to her, "Woman, you are loosed from your infirmity."
- ❧ Jesus laid hands on her.
- ❧ The woman released her faith by standing up straight, doing what she could not do before.

Dear Lord,

You keep all Your covenant promises. You heal the brokenhearted and set the captive free. You loose me from all infirmities, and by Your grace I can stand up straight and tall. Thank You for healing me.

In Jesus' name, Amen.

Jesus Heals Ten Lepers

Now it happened as He went to Jerusalem that He passed through the midst of Samaria and Galilee. Then as He entered a certain village, there met Him ten men who were lepers, who stood afar off. And they lifted up their voices and said, "Jesus, Master, have mercy on us!"

So when He saw them, He said to them, "Go, show yourselves to the priests."

And so it was that as they went, they were cleansed. And one of them, when he saw that he was healed, returned, and with a loud voice glorified God, and fell down on his face at His feet, giving Him thanks. And he was a Samaritan.

So Jesus answered and said, "Were there not ten cleansed? But where are the nine? Were there not any found who returned to give glory to God except this foreigner?" And He said to him, "Arise, go your way. Your faith has made you well." (Luke 17:11-19)

Release of Faith:

- The lepers cried out to Jesus for mercy.
- Jesus said, "Go show yourselves to the priests." Lepers were to show themselves to the priests only if they were cleansed of their leprosy.
- The lepers obeyed, and as they went, they were cleansed.
- One of them returned to give Jesus thanks. Jesus answered, "Your faith has made you well." Faith acknowledges the work of God with thanksgiving.

Dear Lord,
   Thank You for my healing.

In Jesus' name, Amen.

Jesus Heals a Nobleman's Son

So Jesus came again to Cana of Galilee where He had made the water wine. And there was a certain nobleman whose son was sick at Capernaum. When he heard that Jesus had come out of Judea into Galilee, he went to Him and implored Him to come down and heal his son, for he was at the point of death.

Then Jesus said to him, "Unless you people see signs and wonders, you will by no means believe."

The nobleman said to Him, "Sir, come down before my child dies!"

Jesus said to him, "Go your way; your son lives."

So the man believed the word that Jesus spoke to him, and he went his way. And as he was now going down, his servants met him and told him, saying, "Your son lives!"

Then he inquired of them the hour when he got better. And they said to him, "Yesterday at the seventh hour the fever left him." So the father knew that it was at the same hour in which Jesus said to him, "Your son lives." And he himself believed, and his whole household. (John 4:46-53)

Release of Faith:

- ☙ The man asked Jesus to heal his son, and persisted in his request.
- ☙ Jesus answered the man's request, for He is willing to perform healing signs and wonders to encourage the release of faith
- ☙ Jesus said, "Go your way, your son lives." Distance presents no impediment to faith. Jesus simply spoke the word, and the man's son, though distant, was healed.
- ☙ The man believed Jesus' word, went his way, and found that his son was indeed healed.
- ☙ The man came to faith in Jesus Christ, and so did his whole household.

Dear Lord,
    Thank You for sending Your Word to heal me. I receive it now.
                                 In Jesus' name, Amen.

Jesus Heals at the Pool of Bethesda

After this there was a feast of the Jews, and Jesus went up to Jerusalem. Now there is in Jerusalem by the Sheep Gate a pool, which is called in Hebrew, Bethesda, having five porches. In these lay a great multitude of sick people, blind, lame, paralyzed, waiting for the moving of the water. For an angel went down at a certain time into the pool and stirred up the water; then whoever stepped in first, after the stirring of the water, was made well of whatever disease he had.

Now a certain man was there who had an infirmity thirty-eight years. When Jesus saw him lying there, and knew that he already had been in that condition a long time, He said to him, "Do you want to be made well?"

The sick man answered Him, "Sir, I have no man to put me into the pool when the water is stirred up; but while I am coming, another steps down before me."

Jesus said to him, "Rise, take up your bed and walk."

And immediately the man was made well, took up his bed, and walked. (John 5:1-9)

Release of Faith:

- ❧ Jesus asked, "Do you want to be made well?" This was no idle question, for Jesus intended to heal the man.
- ❧ Jesus said, "Rise, take up your bed and walk." Previously, the man had focused on a particular method of healing, but now Jesus focused the man's attention on the Healer.
- ❧ The man obeyed Jesus and did what he could not do before. He took up his bed and walked.

Dear Lord,

Yes, I want to be made well. My focus is on You now, for You are My Healer. In Your name I am made whole—by Your word, by Your blood, and by Your power. Thank You.

In Jesus' name, Amen.

Jesus Heals a Man Blind from Birth

Now as Jesus passed by, He saw a man who was blind from birth. And His disciples asked Him, saying, "Rabbi, who sinned, this man or his parents, that he was born blind?"

Jesus answered, "Neither this man nor his parents sinned, but that the works of God should be revealed in him. I must work the works of Him who sent Me while it is day; the night is coming when no one can work. As long as I am in the world, I am the light of the world."

When He had said these things, He spat on the ground and made clay with the saliva; and He anointed the eyes of the blind man with the clay. And He said to him, "Go, wash in the pool of Siloam" (which is translated, Sent). So he went and washed, and came back seeing. (John 9:1-7)

Release of Faith:

- ✤ Jesus affirmed that healing reveals the works of God.
- ✤ Jesus laid hands on the man, anointing his eyes.
- ✤ Jesus sent the man to wash in the pool of Siloam.
- ✤ The man obeyed Jesus, went and washed, and came back seeing.

Dear Lord,

I thank You that Jesus came to do Your works and that my healing reveals Your glory and goodness. I receive Your healing anointing now.

In Jesus' name, Amen.

Jesus Healed Them All

And Jesus went about all Galilee, teaching in their synagogues, preaching the gospel of the kingdom, and healing all kinds of sickness and all kinds of disease among the people. Then His fame went throughout all Syria; and they brought to Him all sick people who were afflicted with various diseases and torments, and those who were demon-possessed, epileptics, and paralytics; and He healed them. (Matthew 4:23-24)

Then Jesus went about all the cities and villages, teaching in their synagogues, preaching the gospel of the kingdom, and healing every sickness and every disease among the people. (Matthew 9:35)

And when Jesus went out He saw a great multitude; and He was moved with compassion for them, and healed their sick. (Matthew 14:14)

Jesus departed from there, skirted the Sea of Galilee, and went up on the mountain and sat down there. Then great multitudes came to Him, having with them the lame, blind, mute, maimed, and many others; and they laid them down at Jesus' feet, and He healed them. So the multitude marveled when they saw the mute speaking, the maimed made whole, the lame walking, and the blind seeing; and they glorified the God of Israel. (Matthew 15:29-31)

And He came down with them and stood on a level place with a crowd of His disciples and a great multitude of people from all Judea and Jerusalem, and from the seacoast of Tyre and Sidon, who came to hear Him and be healed of their diseases, as well as those who were tormented with unclean spirits. And they were healed. And the whole multitude sought to touch Him, for power went out from Him and healed them all. (Luke 6.:7-19; see also Mark 3:7-10)

And the apostles, when they had returned, told Him all that they had done. Then He took them and went aside privately into a deserted place belonging to the city called Bethsaida. But when the multitudes knew it, they followed Him; and He received them and spoke to them about the kingdom of God, and healed those who had need of healing. (Luke 9:10-11)

Dear Lord Jesus,

In Your earthly ministry, You never turned away anyone who came to You, or was brought to You for healing. But You were moved with compassion and healed those who had need of healing. Whole multitudes came and touched You, and received healing, for healing power went forth from You. You healed every sickness and every disease. You made the lame to walk, the blind to see, the deaf to hear, the mute to speak, and the maimed were made whole. You healed them all!

So Lord, I come to You today for healing, and I believe with all my heart that I will receive it, for You are the same, yesterday, today and forever. Thank You for my healing.

In Jesus' name, Amen.

Signs of the Messiah

Then the disciples of John reported to him concerning all these things. And John, calling two of his disciples to him, sent them to Jesus, saying, "Are You the Coming One, or do we look for another?" When the men had come to Him, they said, "John the Baptist has sent us to You, saying, 'Are You the Coming One, or do we look for another?'"

And that very hour He cured many of infirmities, afflictions, and evil spirits; and to many blind He gave sight. Jesus answered and said to them,

"Go and tell John the things you have seen and heard: that the blind see, the lame walk, the lepers are cleansed, the deaf hear, the dead are raised, the poor have the gospel preached to them. (Luke 7:18-22; see also Matthew 11:1-5)

> Jesus began His ministry announcing that He was anointed by God to preach the Good News to the poor, heal the brokenhearted, give sight to the blind and free the captives. Now nearing the end of His ministry, He presented John with the proof that He is indeed Messiah, the Anointed One.

Many Other Signs

And truly Jesus did many other signs in the presence of His disciples, which are not written in this book; but these are written that you may believe that Jesus is the Christ, the Son of God, and that believing you may have life in His name. (John 20:30,31)

And there are also many other things that Jesus did, which if they were written one by one, I suppose that even the world itself could not contain the books that would be written. (John 21:25)

God anointed Jesus of Nazareth with the Holy Spirit and with power, who went about doing good and healing all who were oppressed by the devil, for God was with Him. (Acts 10:38)

Dear Lord,

Thank You for all Your healing signs and wonders. Thank You for going about doing good, healing all who are oppressed by the devil. Your works are more than can be numbered, and they continue to this day, for You are the same Jesus, now as then. I receive Your signs and I believe that You are the Anointed One, the Son of God. Thank You for the life that I have in You.

In Jesus' name, Amen.

The Healing Ministry of the Disciples

Jesus chose the disciples that they might be with Him—to know Him, love Him, learn of Him, and grow in fellowship with Him. He chose them, also, that He might send them out into the world to preach, to heal and to cast out, or expel demons. He gave them power to do it, He sent them out to do it, and they went out and did it. In this way, He chose to multiply His ministry in the world and thus advance the kingdom of God.

After His resurrection, and before He ascended into heaven, He gave His disciples the Great Commission. He gave them authority and said that they would receive power, the Holy Spirit coming upon them. They were to be witnesses to Him, to preach the Gospel to every person, to make disciples of all the nations, to baptize them, and to teach them to obey and do all that they themselves had received from Jesus. This was, and is, to be a continuing succession of disciples, all doing the works Jesus did, all having authority and power for preaching, healing and deliverance (expelling demons). As they preached the Gospel, there would be signs to follow those who believed. These signs included healing and deliverance—the same things Jesus did. We will see all this in the following accounts, and learn that the ministry of the disciples did indeed include healing and deliverance, as well as other signs and wonders.

Jesus Chooses the Twelve Disciples to Heal

And He went up on the mountain and called to Him those He Himself wanted. And they came to Him. Then He appointed twelve, that they might be with

Him and that He might send them out to preach, and to have power to heal sicknesses and to cast out demons. (Mark 3:13-15)

Jesus Sends Out the Twelve Disciples to Heal

Then Jesus went about all the cities and villages, teaching in their synagogues, preaching the gospel of the kingdom, and healing every sickness and every disease among the people. But when He saw the multitudes, He was moved with compassion for them, because they were weary and scattered, like sheep having no shepherd. Then He said to His disciples, "The harvest truly is plentiful, but the laborers are few. Therefore pray the Lord of the harvest to send out laborers into His harvest."

And when He had called His twelve disciples to Him, He gave them power over unclean spirits, to cast them out, and to heal all kinds of sickness and all kinds of disease. (Matthew 9:35-10:1)

> The full significance of this passage is sometimes lost because of the chapter division in the middle. But the Scriptures were not written with chapter and verse divisions. Those were added later.
>
> Pay close attention to the sequence. Jesus said, "The harvest truly is plentiful, but the laborers are few. Therefore pray the Lord of the harvest to send out laborers into His harvest." Then the very next thing we see is Jesus, the Lord of the Harvest, sending out laborers into His harvest.
>
> Who are the laborers He sends into the harvest? The disciples.
>
> What does He send them to do? Heal all kinds of sickness and all kinds of diseases, and perform deliverance.
>
> This is why He chose them, and this is what He sent them out to do.

These twelve Jesus sent out and commanded them, saying, "And as you go, preach, saying, 'The kingdom of heaven is at hand.' Heal the sick, cleanse the lepers, raise the dead, cast out demons." (Matthew 10:5, 7-8)

And He called the twelve to Himself, and began to send them out two by two, and gave them power over unclean spirits. ... So they went out and preached that people should repent. And they cast out many demons, and anointed with oil many who were sick, and healed them. (Mark 6:7, 12-13)

Then He called His twelve disciples together and gave them power and authority over all demons, and to cure diseases. He sent them to preach the kingdom of God and to heal the sick ... So they departed and went through the towns, preaching the gospel and healing everywhere. (Luke 9:1-2, 6)

Jesus Sends Out the Seventy to Heal

After these things the Lord appointed seventy others also, and sent them two by two before His face into every city and place where He Himself was about to go ... "Whatever city you enter, and they receive you, eat such things as are set before you. And heal the sick there, and say to them, 'The kingdom of God has come near to you." ... Then the seventy returned with joy, saying, 'Lord, even the demons are subject to us in Your name.'" (Luke 10:1, 8-9, 17)

The Disciples Empowered and Commissioned for Healing

And Jesus came and spoke to them, saying, "All authority has been given to Me in heaven and on earth. Go therefore and make disciples of all the nations, baptizing them in the name of the Father and of the Son and of the Holy Spirit, teaching them to observe all things that I have commanded you; and lo, I am with you always, even to the end of the age." (Matthew 28:18-20)

> Jesus announced that all authority had been given to Him, and He delegated that authority to the disciples in the Great Commission. The disciples were to go and make disciples of all nations, teaching them whatever Jesus had taught, including healing and deliverance.

And He said to them, "Go into all the world and preach the gospel to every creature. He who believes and is baptized will be saved; but he who does not believe will be condemned. And these signs will follow those who believe: In My name they will cast out demons; they will speak with new tongues; they will take up serpents; and if they drink anything deadly, it will by no means hurt them; they will lay hands on the sick, and they will recover." (Mark 16:15-18)

> Healing and deliverance belong to all those who are disciples of the Lord Jesus Christ—not only the right to be healed and delivered, but also the authority to minister healing and deliverance to others. These things will follow those

who believe, if those who believe are willing to do what Jesus said.

Most assuredly, I say to you, he who believes in Me, the works that I do he will do also; and greater works than these he will do, because I go to My Father. And whatever you ask in My name, that I will do, that the Father may be glorified in the Son. If you ask anything in My name, I will do it. (John 14:12-14)

> This is true for whoever believes in Jesus. They will be able to do His works—even greater works. This is because, when Jesus ascended into heaven, He would send them the Holy Spirit, who would empower them for these works. What were these works? Preaching, healing and deliverance.

Then He said to them, "Thus it is written, and thus it was necessary for the Christ to suffer and to rise from the dead the third day, and that repentance and remission of sins should be preached in His name to all nations, beginning at Jerusalem. And you are witnesses of these things. Behold, I send the Promise of My Father upon you; but tarry in the city of Jerusalem until you are endued with power from on high." (Luke 24:46-49)

But you shall receive power when the Holy Spirit has come upon you; and you shall be witnesses to Me in Jerusalem, and in all Judea and Samaria, and to the end of the earth. (Acts 1:8)

> The Holy Spirit would come upon the disciples, not just the Twelve, but all of them. This was the Promise of the Father. And they would be endued with power. They had received authority to preach, heal and do deliverance just before Jesus ascended to heaven. Now they would receive power when the Holy Spirit came upon them. This is the same power by which Jesus healed and performed deliverance.
>
> The purpose of this Holy Spirit power is to be a witness to Jesus. A witness is one who presents evidence or proof. Witnesses to Jesus present proof that He is truly the Anointed One—the Messiah. We do this by preaching what Jesus preached and doing what Jesus did, which included healing and deliverance.

The Disciples Perform Many Signs and Wonders

Then fear came upon every soul, and many wonders and signs were done through the apostles. (Acts 2:43)

> Luke's use of "signs and wonders" terminology relates back to Joel's prophecy, which was cited earlier in Acts 2: "I will show wonders in heaven above, and signs in the earth beneath" (v. 19). In the book of Acts, "signs and wonders" generally refers to healing and deliverance.

Peter and John Heal a Lame Man

Now Peter and John went up together to the temple at the hour of prayer, the ninth hour. And a certain man lame from his mother's womb was carried, whom they laid daily at the gate of the temple which is called Beautiful, to ask alms from those who entered the temple; who, seeing Peter and John about to go into the temple, asked for alms.

And fixing his eyes on him, with John, Peter said, "Look at us."

So he gave them his attention, expecting to receive something from them.

Then Peter said, "Silver and gold I do not have, but what I do have I give you: In the name of Jesus Christ of Nazareth, rise up and walk."

And he took him by the right hand and lifted him up, and immediately his feet and ankle bones received strength. So he, leaping up, stood and walked and entered the temple with them—walking, leaping, and praising God.

And all the people saw him walking and praising God. Then they knew that it was he who sat begging alms at the Beautiful Gate of the temple; and they were filled with wonder and amazement at what had happened to him. (Acts 3:1-10)

Release of Faith:

- Peter said, "What I do have I give you." He fully intended to give healing to the lame man.
- Peter said, "In the name of Jesus Christ." He released the power and authority of Jesus' name.
- Peter said, "Rise up and walk." He fully expected the man to be healed and told him to do what he could not do before.

    ▾ The man believed and obeyed what Peter said. He leaped up, stood
       up and walked.

Now as the lame man who was healed held on to Peter and John, all the people
ran together to them in the porch which is called Solomon's, greatly amazed.
So when Peter saw it, he responded to the people: "Men of Israel, why do you
marvel at this? Or why look so intently at us, as though by our own power or
godliness we had made this man walk? The God of Abraham, Isaac, and Jacob,
the God of our fathers, glorified His Servant Jesus ... And His name, through
faith in His name, has made this man strong, whom you see and know. Yes,
the faith which comes through Him has given him this perfect soundness in
the presence of you all. (Acts 3:11-13, 16)

> This healing was performed by the power of God, in the name of Jesus, and
> through faith in His name. In fact, it was by the faith which comes through
> Jesus—the same faith by which Jesus ministered healing to others.

The Disciples Pray for Healing

Now, Lord ... grant to Your servants that with all boldness they may speak
Your word, by stretching out Your hand to heal, and that signs and wonders
may be done through the name of Your holy Servant Jesus.

    And when they had prayed, the place where they were assembled together
was shaken; and they were all filled with the Holy Spirit, and they spoke the
word of God with boldness. (Acts 4:29-31)

> Here again we see the power of the Holy Spirit for preaching (with
> boldness), healing and deliverance. The terminology of signs and wonders
> includes healing, deliverance, and other miracles.

The Disciples Perform Healing Signs and Wonders

And through the hands of the apostles many signs and wonders were done
among the people. And they were all with one accord in Solomon's Porch. Yet
none of the rest dared join them, but the people esteemed them highly.

    And believers were increasingly added to the Lord, multitudes of both
men and women, so that they brought the sick out into the streets and laid

them on beds and couches, that at least the shadow of Peter passing by might fall on some of them. Also a multitude gathered from the surrounding cities to Jerusalem, bringing sick people and those who were tormented by unclean spirits, and they were all healed. (Acts 5:12-16)

> Notice the transfer of healing power, even through the shadow of Peter (perhaps representing the proximity of Peter's healing authority). This is similar to the transfer of healing power which came forth from Jesus even through His garment.
>
> Notice, too, that they *all* were healed. The disciples had the same anointing, power and authority as Jesus did, and so they were seeing the same kind of results Jesus did.

Stephen, a Deacon, Performs Signs and Wonders

And Stephen, full of faith and power, did great wonders and signs among the people. (Acts 6:8)

Philip, a Deacon, Performs Healing Signs and Wonders

Then Philip went down to the city of Samaria and preached Christ to them. And the multitudes with one accord heeded the things spoken by Philip, hearing and seeing the miracles which he did. For unclean spirits, crying with a loud voice, came out of many who were possessed; and many who were paralyzed and lame were healed. And there was great joy in that city. (Acts 8:5-8)

Ananias Heals Saul (Paul) of Blindness

Now there was a certain disciple at Damascus named Ananias; and to him the Lord said in a vision, "Ananias."

And he said, "Here I am, Lord."

So the Lord said to him, "Arise and go to the street called Straight, and inquire at the house of Judas for one called Saul of Tarsus, for behold, he is praying. And in a vision he has seen a man named Ananias coming in and putting his hand on him, so that he might receive his sight."

... And Ananias went his way and entered the house; and laying his hands on him he said, "Brother Saul, the Lord Jesus, who appeared to you on the road as you came, has sent me that you may receive your sight and be filled with the Holy Spirit."

Immediately there fell from his eyes something like scales, and he received his sight at once; and he arose and was baptized. So when he had received food, he was strengthened. Then Saul spent some days with the disciples at Damascus. (Acts 9:10-12, 17-19)

Release of Faith:

- ✢ Ananias believed the vision and obeyed the Lord.
- ✢ Ananias found Paul and laid his hands on him.
- ✢ Ananias spoke what he had heard from the Lord, "The Lord Jesus has sent me that you may receive your sight and be filled with the Holy Spirit."

Peter Heals Aeneas, a Paralytic

Now it came to pass, as Peter went through all parts of the country, that he also came down to the saints who dwelt in Lydda. There he found a certain man named Aeneas, who had been bedridden eight years and was paralyzed.

And Peter said to him, "Aeneas, Jesus the Christ heals you. Arise and make your bed."

Then he arose immediately. So all who dwelt at Lydda and Sharon saw him and turned to the Lord. (Acts 9:32-34)

Release of Faith:

- ✢ Peter said, "Jesus the Christ heals you." He focused Aeneas' attention on Jesus—the source of all healing—and had no doubt that Jesus would indeed heal him.
- ✢ Peter said, "Arise and make your bed." He expected Aeneas to be healed and told him to do what he could not do before.
- ✢ Aeneas obeyed and arose immediately.

The Disciples Do Many Signs and Wonders

Therefore they stayed there a long time, speaking boldly in the Lord, who was bearing witness to the word of His grace, granting signs and wonders to be done by their hands. (Acts 14:3)

Release of Faith:

- The disciples spoke boldly in the Lord.
- They performed signs and wonders.

Paul Heals a Lame Man

And in Lystra a certain man without strength in his feet was sitting, a cripple from his mother's womb, who had never walked. This man heard Paul speaking.

Paul, observing him intently and seeing that he had faith to be healed, said with a loud voice, "Stand up straight on your feet!"

And he leaped and walked. (Acts 14:8-10)

Release of Faith:

- The man possessed faith, as Paul perceived, but he needed to put it in action.
- Paul discerned that the man had faith, and he acted on that discernment.
- Paul said, "Stand up straight on your feet!" By having him do what he could not do before, he gave the man a tangible way to exercise his faith.
- The man obeyed, leaped up and walked.

Paul Heals Many by Handkerchiefs and Aprons

Now God worked unusual miracles by the hands of Paul, so that even handkerchiefs or aprons were brought from his body to the sick, and the diseases left them and the evil spirits went out of them. (Acts 19:11-12)

Just as there were many who touched the hem of Jesus' garment and were healed, healing power transferred also from Paul through his garments.

Paul Heals Many on the Island of Malta

In that region there was an estate of the leading citizen of the island, whose name was Publius, who received us and entertained us courteously for three days. And it happened that the father of Publius lay sick of a fever and dysentery. Paul went in to him and prayed, and he laid his hands on him and healed him. So when this was done, the rest of those on the island who had diseases also came and were healed. (Acts 28:7-9)

Release of Faith:

- ❧ Paul went to Publius' father and prayed.
- ❧ Paul laid hands on him and healed him.
- ❧ The rest of those who had diseases came, and were healed.

These Signs will Follow

The Great Commission is still in effect and fully operative today. The authority of Jesus and the powerful anointings of the Holy Spirit remain in the church:

- ❧ to preach the Gospel to everyone
- ❧ to make disciples of all nations
- ❧ to baptize them
- ❧ to teach them everything Jesus taught the first disciples
- ❧ to do the works of Jesus
- ❧ to be witnesses of Jesus
- ❧ to lay hands on the sick and heal them
- ❧ to expel demons

Jesus has chosen us to be with Him. As we begin to know Him, love Him, learn from Him, and grow in fellowship with Him, we should expect to see healing and deliverance happen more and more. We should expect, not only to receive these things for ourselves, but to be discipled in how to minister them to others.

And these signs will follow those who believe: In My name they will cast out demons ... They will lay hands on the sick, and they will recover. (Mark 16:17-18)

Raising the Dead

The Bible records a number of accounts in which someone who died was restored to life. Elijah brought the widow of Zaraphath's son back to life (1 Kings 17:17-24). When the son of a Shunnamite woman died, Elisha raised him from the dead (2 Kings 4:25-37). A dead man who was thrown into Elisha's grave was restored to life when his body came into contact with the bones of Elisha (2 Kings 13:20-21).

Properly speaking, these were all resuscitations. Each one of these persons actually died and was restored to life, but these were not resurrections, not in the biblical sense. In the Bible, the resurrection of God's people refers, not merely to the restoration of life, but more importantly, it speaks of the transformation and glorification of the body. Resurrection indicates immortality. Those who are merely resuscitated eventually die again, but those who are resurrected will never die again.

In 1 Corinthians 15, the apostle Paul teaches on the significance of the resurrection of the Lord Jesus Christ from the dead and how that guarantees the resurrection of all those who believe in Him.

> But now Christ is risen from the dead, and has become the firstfruits of those who have fallen asleep. For since by man came death, by Man also came the resurrection of the dead. For as in Adam all die, even so in Christ all shall be made alive. But each one in his own order: Christ the firstfruits, afterward those who are Christ's at His coming. Then comes the end, when He delivers the kingdom to God the Father,

when He puts an end to all rule and all authority and power. For He must reign till He has put all enemies under His feet. The last enemy that will be destroyed is death. (1 Corinthians 15:20-26).

The Bible says, "But if the Spirit of Him who raised Jesus from the dead dwells in you, He who raised Christ from the dead will also give life to your mortal bodies through His Spirit who dwells in you" (Romans 8:11). The Spirit of God, whose power raised the Lord Jesus Christ from the dead, will one day give resurrection life to our bodies as well. But that same Spirit also dwells in us today. His power is now present in us and is able to bring life and health to our bodies.

The following New Testament accounts are resuscitation stories—the dead being raised to life, but not necessarily to immortality. They are included in this book because they deal with the end result of sickness and disease—which is death. They encourage us that there is no sickness, disease or any other condition that is too difficult for God to deal with. He is able to restore the health of a person fully and completely, even when the very breath of life has departed. The power of God that raises the dead is the very same power that heals the sick.

Enlarge your expectation. In the Old Testament, a few dead were raised to life. In the New Testament, many more were restored. In fact, Jesus sent His disciples to "heal the sick, cleanse the lepers, *raise the dead*, cast out demons" (Matthew 10.8). At the Great Commission, He charged them to make other disciples, "teaching them to observe all things that I have commanded you" (Matthew 28.20). This would include raising the dead—nothing in the words of Jesus leaves it out. In fact, Jesus said, "He who believes in Me, the works that I do he will do also; and greater works than these he will do, because I go to My Father" (John 14:12).

Jesus and His disciples raised the dead, and many other restoration accounts have been recorded in the history of the Church, particularly in the last century. We should expect to see this happen more and more.

Jesus Raises a Widow's Son Back to Life

Now it happened, the day after, that He went into a city called Nain; and many of His disciples went with Him, and a large crowd. And when He came near the gate of the city, behold, a dead man was being carried out, the only son of his mother; and she was a widow. And a large crowd from the city was with her.

When the Lord saw her, He had compassion on her and said to her, "Do not weep."

Then He came and touched the open coffin, and those who carried him stood still. And He said, "Young man, I say to you, arise."

So he who was dead sat up and began to speak. And He presented him to his mother. (Luke 7:11-15)

Release of Faith:

- ↪ Jesus said, "Do not weep," for He intended to raise the woman's son back to life.
- ↪ Jesus touched the coffin, even though this would have been considered ceremonially unclean. This was not an idle touch, for He intended to raise the young man back to life.
- ↪ Jesus spoke the word of command, "Young man, I say to you, arise."

Raising the Dead Shows that Jesus is the Anointed One

And that very hour He cured many of infirmities, afflictions, and evil spirits; and to many blind He gave sight. Jesus answered and said to them, "Go and tell John the things you have seen and heard: that the blind see, the lame walk, the lepers are cleansed, the deaf hear, the dead are raised, the poor have the gospel preached to them. (Luke 7:22)

Jesus Raises the Daughter of Jairus Back to Life

So it was, when Jesus returned, that the multitude welcomed Him, for they were all waiting for Him. And behold, there came a man named Jairus, and he was a ruler of the synagogue. And he fell down at Jesus' feet and begged Him to come to his house, for he had an only daughter about twelve years of age, and she was dying ...

Someone came from the ruler of the synagogue's house, saying to him, "Your daughter is dead. Do not trouble the Teacher."

But when Jesus heard it, He answered him, saying, "Do not be afraid; only believe, and she will be made well."

When He came into the house, He permitted no one to go in except Peter, James, and John, and the father and mother of the girl. Now all wept and mourned for her; but He said, "Do not weep; she is not dead, but sleeping."

And they ridiculed Him, knowing that she was dead. But He put them all outside, took her by the hand and called, saying, "Little girl, arise."

Then her spirit returned, and she arose immediately. And He commanded that she be given something to eat. And her parents were astonished, but He charged them to tell no one what had happened. (Luke 8:40-56)

Release of Faith:

- Jairus came to Jesus, asking Him to come to his house, with the expectation that his daughter would be healed.
- When Jairus' servants brought news of his daughter's death, Jesus told him, "Do not be afraid; only believe, and she will be made well."
- Jairus obeyed, for he continued bringing Jesus to his daughter.
- Jesus said, "Do not weep; she is not dead, but sleeping." Then He eliminated all unbelief from the room.
- Jesus laid hands on the girl and said, "Little girl, arise."

Jesus Raises Lazarus Back to Life

Now a certain man was sick, Lazarus of Bethany, the town of Mary and her sister Martha. It was that Mary who anointed the Lord with fragrant oil and wiped His feet with her hair, whose brother Lazarus was sick. Therefore the sisters sent to Him, saying, "Lord, behold, he whom You love is sick." When Jesus heard that, He said, "This sickness is not unto death, but for the glory of God, that the Son of God may be glorified through it." Now Jesus loved Martha and her sister and Lazarus. So, when He heard that he was sick, He stayed two more days in the place where He was ...

After that He said to them [His disciples], "Our friend Lazarus sleeps, but I go that I may wake him up."

Then His disciples said, "Lord, if he sleeps he will get well."

However, Jesus spoke of his death, but they thought that He was speaking about taking rest in sleep. Then Jesus said to them plainly, "Lazarus is dead. And I am glad for your sakes that I was not there, that you may believe. Nevertheless let us go to him."

So when Jesus came, He found that he had already been in the tomb four days ... Then Martha, as soon as she heard that Jesus was coming, went and met Him, but Mary was sitting in the house.

Then Martha said to Jesus, "Lord, if You had been here, my brother would not have died. But even now I know that whatever You ask of God, God will give You."

Jesus said to her, "Your brother will rise again."

Martha said to Him, "I know that he will rise again in the resurrection at the last day."

Jesus said to her, "I am the resurrection and the life. He who believes in Me, though he may die, he shall live. "And whoever lives and believes in Me shall never die. Do you believe this?"

She said to Him, "Yes, Lord, I believe that You are the Christ, the Son of God, who is to come into the world."

... When Mary came where Jesus was, and saw Him, she fell down at His feet, saying to Him, "Lord, if You had been here, my brother would not have died." Therefore, when Jesus saw her weeping, and the Jews who came with her weeping, He groaned in the spirit and was troubled.

And He said, "Where have you laid him?"

They said to Him, "Lord, come and see."

Jesus wept.

Then the Jews said, "See how He loved him!" And some of them said, "Could not this Man, who opened the eyes of the blind, also have kept this man from dying?"

Then Jesus, again groaning in Himself, came to the tomb. It was a cave, and a stone lay against it. Jesus said, "Take away the stone."

Martha, the sister of him who was dead, said to Him, "Lord, by this time there is a stench, for he has been dead four days."

Jesus said to her, "Did I not say to you that if you would believe you would see the glory of God?" Then they took away the stone from the place where the dead man was lying. And Jesus lifted up His eyes and said, "Father, I thank You that You have heard Me. And I know that You always hear Me, but because of the people who are standing by I said this, that they may believe that You sent Me."

Now when He had said these things, He cried with a loud voice, "Lazarus, come forth!" And he who had died came out bound hand and foot with grave clothes, and his face was wrapped with a cloth. Jesus said to them, "Loose him, and let him go." (John 11:1-45)

Release of faith:

- ❧ Jesus said from the beginning, "This sickness is not unto death."
- ❧ Knowing that Lazarus was dead, Jesus said to the disciples, "Our friend Lazarus sleeps, but I go that I may wake him up."
- ❧ Jesus said, "Lazarus is dead ... Nevertheless let us go to him."
- ❧ Jesus said to Martha, "Your brother will rise again."
- ❧ Jesus said to Martha, "He who lives and believes in Me shall never die." Then He drew out Martha's faith by asking, "Do you believe this?"
- ❧ Martha released her faith and said to Jesus, "Yes, Lord, I believe that You are the Christ."
- ❧ Jesus had the stone removed from the tomb so Lazarus could come forth.
- ❧ Jesus reiterated His earlier words to Martha, "If you believe you will see the glory of God."
- ❧ Jesus gave thanks to God and declared His faith. "Father, I thank You that You have heard Me. And I know that You always hear me."
- ❧ Jesus cried out, "Lazarus, come forth."
- ❧ When Lazarus came forth, Jesus said, "Loose him, and let him go." Lazarus was alive and free.

Jesus Sends Out the Disciples to Raise the Dead

These twelve Jesus sent out and commanded them, saying, "And as you go, preach, saying, 'The kingdom of heaven is at hand.' Heal the sick, cleanse the lepers, raise the dead, cast out demons." (Matthew 10:5, 7-8)

Release of faith: Jesus sent the disciples out with the expectation that they would heal the sick, cleanse the lepers, raise the dead, and cast out demons.

Peter Raises Dorcas Back to Life

At Joppa there was a certain disciple named Tabitha, which is translated Dorcas. This woman was full of good works and charitable deeds which she did. But it happened in those days that she became sick and died. When they had washed her, they laid her in an upper room. And since Lydda was near Joppa, and the disciples had heard that Peter was there, they sent two men to him, imploring him not to delay in coming to them.

Then Peter arose and went with them. When he had come, they brought him to the upper room. And all the widows stood by him weeping, showing the tunics and garments which Dorcas had made while she was with them. But Peter put them all out, and knelt down and prayed.

And turning to the body he said, "Tabitha, arise."

And she opened her eyes, and when she saw Peter she sat up. Then he gave her his hand and lifted her up; and when he had called the saints and widows, he presented her alive. And it became known throughout all Joppa, and many believed on the Lord. (Acts 9:36-42)

Release of faith:

- When Dorcas died, two men went to Peter, asking him to come without delay. The body would have to be buried by the end of the day. They had an expectation that Peter could do something, even though the time was short.
- Peter arose and went with them. He had an expectation that he could do something in this situation.
- When Peter arrived, he cleared the room of unbelief.
- Peter spoke to the body, and calling her by name said, "Tabitha, Arise."
- When she opened her eyes and sat up, Peter followed through by taking her hand, lifting her up, and presenting her to her friends. Not only was she restored to life, she was restored to strength and was able to rise and walk.

Paul Brings Eutychus Back to Life

Now on the first day of the week, when the disciples came together to break bread, Paul, ready to depart the next day, spoke to them and continued his message until midnight. There were many lamps in the upper room where they were gathered together. And in a window sat a certain young man named Eutychus, who was sinking into a deep sleep. He was overcome by sleep; and as Paul continued speaking, he fell down from the third story and was taken up dead.

But Paul went down, fell on him, and embracing him said, "Do not trouble yourselves, for his life is in him."

Now when he had come up, had broken bread and eaten, and talked a long while, even till daybreak, he departed.

And they brought the young man in alive, and they were not a little comforted. (Acts 20:7-12)

Release of faith:

- Paul threw himself on the boy and embraced him, in a manner similar to the way Elijah and Elisha raised the sons of the widows back to life.
- Paul said, "His life is in him," and the boy was well.

Dear Lord,

Nothing is too difficult for You: You heal the sick, cleanse the lepers, raise the dead, cast out demons. The Holy Spirit of God, who raised the Lord Jesus Christ from the dead now dwells inside me. His power is now present to give me life and health. I receive His healing work now.

In Jesus' name, Amen.

The Healing Name of Jesus

The name of the Lord Jesus Christ signifies healing in a number of ways. First, there is authority in His name. Jesus said, "Most assuredly, I say to you, whatever you ask the Father in My name He will give you. Until now you have asked nothing in My name. Ask, and you will receive, that your joy may be full" (John 16:23-24).

Whatever we ask the Father in the name of Jesus, He will give us. To ask in Jesus' name means to ask according to His purposes, to ask as He would ask. The earthly ministry of Jesus reveals that His purpose and will regarding sickness and disease is to heal. He never turned away anyone who came to Him for healing, but healed them all. Therefore, when we ask for healing in the name of Jesus, we are asking as He would ask and in accordance with His will.

When the disciples healed, they did it in the name of Jesus. For example, Peter said to the lame man, "In the name of Jesus Christ of Nazareth, rise up and walk" (Acts 3:6). When the man jumped up and began to walk and leap and praise God, a crowd started to gather. Using this as an opportunity to preach, Peter went on to tell them about Jesus. "And His name, through faith in His name, has made this man strong, whom you see and know. Yes, the faith which comes through Him has given him this perfect soundness in the presence of you all" (Acts 3:16-17).

The name of Jesus is wonderful. The Bible says, "Your name is ointment poured forth" (Song of Solomon 1:3). "Whoever calls on the name of the LORD shall be saved" (Romans 10:13). "Believe on the Lord Jesus Christ, and you will be saved" (Acts 16:31). Let us consider the name of the Lord Jesus Christ more closely.

He is Lord

If you confess with your mouth Jesus as Lord, and believe in your heart that God raised Him from the dead, you will be saved. (Romans 10:9 *NASB*)

Therefore God also has highly exalted Him and given Him the name which is above every name, that at the name of Jesus every knee should bow, of those in heaven, and of those on earth, and of those under the earth, and that every tongue should confess that Jesus Christ is Lord, to the glory of God the Father. (Philippians 2:9-11).

> Jesus is Lord! God has raised Him from the dead and seated Him at His right hand in the heavenlies, "far above all principality and power and might and dominion, and every name that is named, not only in this age but also in that which is to come" (Ephesians 1:21).
>
> The Lordship of Jesus signifies our healing, for He is seated far above every sickness. He has authority over every disease. They are all under His feet. When we confess His name in healing prayer, we are exercising His authority over sickness and disease, and they must line up under His Lordship.

His Name is Jesus

And she will bring forth a son, and you shall call His name Jesus, for He will save His people from their sins. (Matthew 1:21).

> The name Jesus is the Greek form of the Hebrew word yeshua, which means "salvation." In the Old Testament, yeshua is used to refer to deliverance, aid, victory, prosperity, help, welfare, healing and health. How it is used in any specific instance depends upon what the need is. Where there is sin, salvation is forgiveness. Where there is an enemy, salvation is deliverance. Where there is lack or want, salvation is prosperity. Where there is sickness, salvation is healing. Salvation is wonderful—it takes care of all our needs. That is why the name of Jesus is so precious, because it literally means salvation.
>
> The son Mary brought forth at Bethlemen was called Jesus, "for He will save His people from their sins." The Greek word for "save" is *sozo*,

and like the Old Testament word for salvation, it means to save, to heal, to deliver, to make whole. Jesus saves us from our sins, from the bondage of our sins, from the penalty of our sins.

> Surely He has borne our griefs [literally "sicknesses"] and carried our sorrows [literally "pains"]; yet we esteemed Him stricken, smitten by God, and afflicted. But He was wounded for our transgressions, He was bruised for our iniquities; the chastisement for our peace was upon Him, and by His stripes we are healed. (Isaiah 53:4-5)

He is the Christ

And it shall come to pass in that day, that his burden shall be taken away from off thy shoulder, and his yoke from off thy neck, and the yoke shall be destroyed because of the anointing. (Isaiah 10:27 *KJV*)

The name *Christ* is the Greek equivalent of the Hebrew *Messiah* and means, "Anointed One." In the Old Testament, there was a special anointing for kings and priests which foreshadowed one especially anointed by God, who would one day arrive on the scene and deliver His people. Jesus is that Anointed One. He is our King, exalted to the throne, and ruling and reigning at the right hand of the Father. He is our High Priest, who ever lives to make intercession for us before the Father.

The anointing is a very powerful thing—it lifts the burden off of us and completely destroys the yoke. The anointing of Jesus is healing for us—it removes the burden of sickness and destroys the yoke of disease in our lives. "God anointed Jesus of Nazareth with the Holy Spirit and with power, who went about doing good and healing all who were oppressed by the devil, for God was with Him" (Acts 10:38).

Dear Lord Jesus Christ,

Every knee shall bow and every tongue shall confess that You are Lord. Your name is above every name and You are seated far above every principality, power, might and dominion. You have authority over every sickness and disease, to bring forth health and wholeness in my life. You are my Lord.

O Jesus, Your very name is my deliverance, my healing, my help, my victory and my prosperity. You save me from my sins. You bore my sicknesses and my pains. You were wounded for my transgressions and bruised for my iniquities. The payment for my peace was upon You. By Your stripes I am healed. You are my Salvation.

You are the Christ, the Messiah, the Anointed One. You are my King, now exalted to the highest throne. You are my High Priest, always before the Father on my behalf. Your anointing removes every burden of sickness and destroys every yoke of disease in my life. You are my Healer.

I will praise You forever and ever.

In Jesus' name, Amen.

The Lord's Prayer as Healing Prayer

The Lord's Prayer is a model Jesus gave to His disciples to teach them how to pray. It is not a list of *what* to pray, but a manner of *how* to pray. It is a framework of how to come and present ourselves before the Lord and lay hold of His promises. It can be used in any circumstance and to meet many needs. Here, of course, we are exploring it in the context of healing prayer.

A woman once asked her spiritual mentor to help her learn how to pray. He answered, "Pray the Lord's Prayer, but take an hour to do it." That may seem difficult, but it really isn't because you have the Holy Spirit to help you.

When you begin, don't be in a hurry. Take your time and pray slowly. As you do, you may find that you feel an inward desire to expand upon some particular point. That is the Holy Spirit prompting you, and if you listen carefully, He will give you words to pray back to the Father. Go with this as far as the Spirit leads you. When you come to the end, sit quietly and contemplate what the Spirit has given you. If you wish, you can pick up the prayer where you left off, and continue until the Spirit gives you more. When you come to the end of your devotional time, simply give thanks and praise to God and welcome His healing power at work in your life.

Our Father in Heaven

God is our faithful Father. He gives only good things to His children. "Every good gift and every perfect gift is from above, and comes down from the Father of lights, with whom there is no variation or shadow of turning" (James 1:17).

> Or what man is there among you who, if his son asks for bread, will give him a stone? Or if he asks for a fish, will he give him a serpent? If you then, being evil, know how to give good gifts to your children, how much more will your Father who is in heaven give good things to those who ask Him! (Matthew 7:9-11)

Our Father in heaven will give good things to His children, but notice that He gives them to those who *ask*. That is how we appropriate the good things of God, by asking. When you ask, ask in faith, expecting to receive only good things from God. He will not give you something that looks good, but is really evil or bad.

Healing is a good thing; sickness is a bad thing. When you ask for healing, expect healing. Do not expect sickness to remain.

Hallowed be Your Name

The word "hallow" is the verb form of "holy." To hallow something means to sanctify it, to set it apart as holy. God and His name are already holy, so the prayer here is that His name would be seen and recognized for the uniquely holy thing that it is. Let God be glorified in heaven and on earth. Let His name be fully appreciated. Let His greatness and goodness be received and honored everywhere.

As we have seen, God has revealed Himself by many names which have a healing benefit. For example:

- ❧ *The LORD Who Heals.* He is my healer.
- ❧ *The LORD Will Provide.* He has seen my need and has provided for my healing.
- ❧ *The LORD My Banner.* He is my victory over sin, sickness and everything that stands against me.
- ❧ *The LORD My Peace.* He is my wholeness, in Him I am made complete.
- ❧ *The LORD My Shepherd.* He takes care of me and I do not lack any good thing.
- ❧ *The LORD My Righteousness.* He qualifies me to receive every blessing and promise of God.

These and many other names show the holiness of God. No one else is like the Lord; no one else can do the things He can do. As you pray this prayer, let these names become holy in your own heart. Honor these names and receive them into your being. Give glory to Him by these names, affirming all their healing significance.

Your Kingdom Come

The Greek tense of this verb, "come," refers to a constant or continuing action. The kingdom of God has already begun, but we look for it to keep coming until it is here in all its fullness.

Healing is a sign of God's kingdom. That is why the Bible says that, when the multitudes came to Jesus, He received them and spoke to them about the kingdom of God, and then healed those who needed healing (Luke 9:11). Later, when Jesus sent the Seventy out to minister, He instructed them, "Whatever city you enter, and they receive you … heal the sick there, and say to them, 'The kingdom of God has come near to you'" (Luke 10:8-9).

Your Will be Done on Earth as it is in Heaven

The kingdom of God is His rule and reign, His will being done on earth as it is in heaven. The phrase "Your will be done" refers to a continuing action. We look for God's will to be done more and more on the earth.

In this prayer, Jesus gives us authority to bring heaven on earth. We find this same authority presented differently in another place:

Assuredly, I say to you, whatever you bind on earth will be bound in heaven, and whatever you loose on earth will be loosed in heaven. Again I say to you that if two of you agree on earth concerning anything that they ask, it will be done for them by My Father in heaven. (Matthew 18:18-19)

The Greek tense of "will be bound" actually means "will have already been bound." Likewise for "will be loosed." In other words, by our binding and loosing, we are doing what has already been done in heaven. We are causing the will of God to be done on earth as it is in heaven.

The power of agreement brings the things of heaven to earth. When we agree on earth concerning anything we ask, it will be done for us by our Father in heaven.

When you pray this prayer, remember that, as one who has received the Lord Jesus Christ and has been born again, you are a citizen of heaven (Philippians 3:20). What is more, the Bible says that you are now seated with the Lord Jesus Christ in the heavenlies (Ephesians 2:6). This means that we do not bring heaven *down* to earth—we bring it *forth*! The kingdom of God does not so much come *to* us as it does *through* us.

All of this is important in regard to healing, for this simple reason—there is no sickness in heaven! Sickness is not God's will in heaven, nor it is His will upon the earth. Therefore, when we pray, "Your will be done on earth as it is in heaven," we can apply that to healing and expect to see it happen.

Give us this Day our Daily Bread

God is committed to meeting our needs every day. This petition certainly brings that out, but there is also a greater dynamic at work. The Greek word for "daily" here is *epiousios*. Many Bible commentators believe that it actually means "for the morrow." This is supported by the use of a related word, *epiouse*, translated in Acts 7:26 and Acts 16:11 as "the next day." In other words, "daily bread" is the bread of tomorrow.

Remember that this is a prayer concerning the kingdom of God, which is now breaking into the world. As God's children, we have access to its blessings and benefits, so in this request we ask God to give us the bread of tomorrow—not of the next twenty-four hour period, but of that day when God's kingdom fully and completely arrives upon the earth. It is "kingdom" bread, and we ask to receive it today. It is the provision of heaven, and we ask for it so that God's will may be done on earth as it is in heaven. It is the substance and power of heaven—and it brings healing to us.

Forgive us our Debt, as We Forgive our Debtors

Forgiveness is always an important issue for us. No matter where we are in our spiritual life, no matter what the issue is at hand, we must always forgive. The Lord has given us a great promise regarding prayer, but as great as that promise is, it can be totally blocked if we do not forgive others.

> Therefore I say to you, whatever things you ask when you pray, believe that you receive them, and you will have them. And whenever you stand

praying, if you have anything against anyone, forgive him, that your Father in heaven may also forgive you your trespasses. (Mark 11:24-25)

Anything that can block your prayers from being answered can also block your healing. But when we forgive, we release the healing power of God to flow into our lives. There are many testimonies of people who finally received their healing once they obeyed this command to forgive others. Even deep-seated illnesses disappeared when deeply buried offenses were forgiven.

Do not Lead us into Temptation, but Deliver us from the Evil One

These two phrases go together. Another way to read them might be, "Do not let us fail the test. Deliver us from the evil one and the plans he has for our lives."

The evil one is the devil. But the Bible says, "For this purpose the Son of God was manifested, that He might destroy the works of the devil" (1 John 3:8). Jesus has come for the express purpose of delivering us from the evil one and his works.

Evil is the lack of good. Prosperity, for example, is a good thing, but poverty is an evil thing because it is a lack of resources. Health is a good thing, but sickness is an evil thing because it is a lack of wholeness.

The devil is the evil one because he comes to take away that which is good. Jesus said, "The thief does not come except to steal, and to kill, and to destroy. I have come that they may have life, and that they may have it more abundantly" (John 10:10). The devil comes to steal our health, take our lives and destroy our well-being. But Jesus has come to destroy the works of the devil and give us life that goes beyond all boundaries.

Yours is the Kingdom and the Power and the Glory

The kingdom of God is the rule and reign of God, and it is good because He is good. Sickness has no place in God's kingdom because sickness is lack, and God's rule and reign brings wholeness. Therefore, wherever His kingdom expands, there will be healing.

The power of God is here to fulfill His kingdom purposes. Paul said that the Gospel is the power of God for salvation. It is the power to save, heal, deliver, make whole and preserve.

The glory of God is His greatness and goodness being revealed in the world. God is not glorified by poverty and lack, He is glorified by meeting the need. He is not glorified by sickness, but by healing the sick and bringing them to wholeness.

Our Father in heaven,
Hallowed be Your name.
Your kingdom come.
Your will be done
on earth as it is in heaven.
Give us this day our daily bread.
And forgive us our debts,
as we forgive our debtors.
And do not lead us into temptation,
but deliver us from the evil one.
For Yours is the kingdom
and the power
and the glory forever.
Amen.

The Lord's Supper as Healing Prayer

Healing power flowed from the body of Jesus. When a leper came to Him, Jesus put out His hand and touched him, and his leprosy was cleansed (Matthew 8:1-3). When Peter's mother-in-law was sick with fever, Jesus touched her hand, and the fever left her (Matthew 8:14-15). Others with various diseases were brought to Him—He laid His hands on every one of them and they were healed (Luke 4:40). Blind eyes received their sight when Jesus touched them (Matthew 20:32-34). Deaf ears opened when Jesus put His fingers in them (Mark 7:32-35).

These were the ones whom Jesus touched, but there were also those who came to touch *Him*. The woman with the issue of blood touched the edge of His garment and received her healing (Mark 5:25-34). Healing flowed from His body, for Jesus knew immediately that power had gone out of Him and that someone had touched Him in faith. There were also many others who were healed when they touched the edge of His garment. "And as many as touched it were made perfectly well" (Matthew 14:36).

In the Lord's Supper, God has given us a very wonderful way to lay hold of the healing benefits of the body and blood of Jesus. The woman with the issue of blood touched the edge of Jesus' garment, but at the Lord's Supper we can experience His healing presence in a much more profound way.

The Lord's Supper is an ordinance, commanded and commissioned by Jesus for the Church. It is a sacrament, an outward sign of an inward reality, signifying His presence. It is a means of grace by which God strengthens and

HEALING SCRIPTURES AND PRAYERS

blesses His people. It is called Communion, a prayer of fellowship with the Lord Jesus Christ. Paul gives us this account of it:

> For I received from the Lord that which I also delivered to you: that the Lord Jesus on the same night in which He was betrayed took bread; and when He had given thanks, He broke it and said, "Take, eat; this is My body which is broken for you; do this in remembrance of Me." In the same manner He also took the cup after supper, saying, "This cup is the new covenant in My blood. This do, as often as you drink it, in remembrance of Me." For as often as you eat this bread and drink this cup, you proclaim the Lord's death till He comes. (1 Corinthians 11:23-26)

This is My Body Which is Given for You

Luke 22:19 has "This is my body which is *given* for you." The "breaking" of bread is actually the giving of bread. The body of Jesus was given on the Cross, but it was not broken. "Many are the afflictions of the righteous, but the LORD delivers him out of them all. He guards all his bones; not one of them is broken" (Psalm 34:19-20).

We see this fulfilled in John's account of the Crucifixion. "But when they came to Jesus and saw that He was already dead, they did not break His legs ... For these things were done that the Scripture should be fulfilled, 'Not one of His bones shall be broken'" (John 19:33, 36).

Jesus bore all our afflictions for us, but He was not broken by them, for the Lord delivered Him from them all. Therefore, because He has been delivered, He is able to minister healing and wholeness to us today. Many have experienced this at the Lord's Table.

The New Covenant in My Blood

Luke 22:20 adds, "This cup is the new covenant in My blood, *which is shed for you*." Matthew's account picks up even more: "For this is my blood of the new covenant, which is shed for many for the remission of sins" (Matthew 26:28).

The blood of Jesus was shed for our sins. It is the sign of a new covenant that has been instituted, a better covenant than the old covenant under Moses. "But now He [Jesus] has obtained a more excellent ministry, inasmuch as He is also Mediator of a

114

better covenant, which was established on better promises" (Hebrews 8:6).

The essence of covenant is exchange: Jesus took our sin that we might have His righteousness. "For He [God] made Him [Jesus] who knew no sin to be sin for us, that we might become the righteousness of God in Him" (2 Corinthians 5:21).

Jesus took our curse that we might have His blessing. "Christ has redeemed us from the curse of the law, having become a curse for us (for it is written, 'Cursed is everyone who hangs on a tree'), that the blessing of Abraham might come upon the Gentiles in Christ Jesus" (Galatians 3:13-14).

Jesus took our sickness that we might have His wholeness. "Surely He has borne our griefs [literally "sicknesses"] and carried our sorrows [literally "pains"] ... He was wounded for our transgressions, He was bruised for our iniquities. The chastisement for our peace was upon Him, and by His stripes we are healed" (Isaiah 53:4-5).

For our Sins *and* Sicknesses

Jesus bore our sicknesses and pains in His own body in the same way He bore our sins. "He was numbered with the transgressors and bore the sin of many"(Isaiah 53:12). The Hebrew word for "bore" in each instance is the word *nasa*. It means to lift a burden and carry it far away. When Jesus bore our sins, He lifted them off of us and carried them far away so we could be forgiven. Likewise, when He bore our sicknesses, He lifted them off of us and carried them far away so we could be healed. We receive this healing in the same way we receive forgiveness—by faith.

When we celebrate the Lord's Supper, we receive an outward sign of an inward reality. The sign of the cup shows that forgiveness of sins and the righteousness of Christ belongs to us by His blood. In the same way, the sign of the bread shows that healing belongs to us by His body.

Healing and forgiveness go together, just as the body and the blood go together. The psalm writer said, "Bless the Lord, O my soul, and forget not all His benefits: Who forgives all your iniquities, Who heals all your diseases" (Psalm 103:2-3). Without the forgiveness of sins, there could be no healing of diseases.

In Luke 5, when a paralytic man was let down through the roof that Jesus might heal him, Jesus said, "Your sins are forgiven you" (v. 20). Then, to show that He had the authority to forgive sins, He said, "Arise, take up your bed, and go to your house" (v. 24). Jesus had authority to heal the man of his paralysis because He had the authority to forgive his sins. Both actions were based on the work of the Cross, where He gave His body and shed His blood.

As Often as you Eat this Bread and Drink this Cup

The Lord our Shepherd has prepared a table for you, even in the presence of your enemies. It is the place where all your needs are met. It is the place where you are anointed with fresh oil. It is the place where your cup runs over. It is the place from which the goodness and mercy of God follow you all the days of your life. It is the place where you can dwell in the house of the Lord always. It is the place of your healing.

Take your place at this table. For as often as you eat this bread and drink this cup, you proclaim the Lord's death till He comes. It is for you that He came. It is for you that He died. It is for you that He is coming again.

The Lord's Supper is the sign of your victory in Jesus Christ over sin, sickness and everything that stands against you. You proclaim this victory as often as you take the bread and the cup. Therefore—do it often!

Dear Lord,
Thank You for the blood shed for me.
Thank You for the body given for me.
Thank You for the forgiveness of my sins.
Thank You for the healing of my body.

In Jesus' name, Amen.

Listen to
Healing Scriptures and Prayers
read by Jeff Doles

Sit back and relax as these healing Scriptures and prayers, read by Jeff Doles, wash over you and stir up your faith to receive God's healing promises. The prayers will help you exercise your faith as you present God's Word before Him with joy and expectation. The gentle background music will refresh you as you meditate on the healing Word of God. Adapted from our book, these recordings are great for soaking prayer!

Vol 1: Old Testament Scriptures
Vol 2: New Testament Scriptures
Vol 3: The Healing Names of God
Vol 4: The Healing Ministry of Jesus

Listen to audio previews and order in MP3 or CD online at
www.walkingbarefoot.com

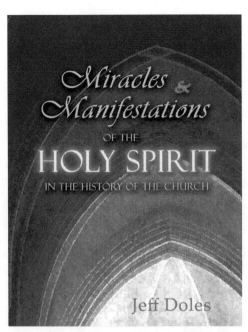

Miracles and Manifestations of the Holy Spirit
in the History of the Church

by Jeff Doles
7.4 x 9.6 in., 274 pages (Paperback)

God has always done miracles in His Church—and still does! The Holy Spirit has never left the Church and neither have His supernatural gifts and manifestations. They have been available in every century—from the days of the Apostolic Fathers, to the desert monks of Egypt and Syria, to the missionary outreaches of the Middle Ages, to the Reformation era and the awakenings and revivals that followed, to the Pentecostal explosion of the Twentieth Century and the increase of signs and wonders in the Twenty-first. Miracles, healings, deliverances, prophecies, dreams, visions—even raising the dead!—have all been in operation throughout the history of the Church. Anglicans, Baptists, Catholics, Congregationalists, Lutherans, Methodists, Moravians, Presbyterians, Quakers and many others have experienced the supernatural gifts and workings of the Spirit over the centuries. *Miracles and Manifestations of the Holy Spirit in the History of the Church* gathers up numerous accounts from a variety of historical sources and provides a handy reference for those who want to know more about how the Church has understood and operated in the gifts and manifestations of the Holy Spirit at various times in history.

6806737R00072

Made in the USA
San Bernardino, CA
15 December 2013